Practice Principles:

Career Theories and Models at Work

Nancy Arthur, Roberta Borgen, Mary McMahon

Practice Principles: Career Theories and Models at Work
Copyright © Nancy Arthur, Roberta Borgen, Mary McMahon (2024)

Published by:
CERIC
Foundation House
Suite 300, 2 St. Clair Avenue East
Toronto, ON
M4T 2T5

Website: www.ceric.ca
Email: admin@ceric.ca

ISBN
Print book: ISBN: 978-1-988066-73-8
eBook ISBN: 978-1-988066-74-5
ePDF: ISBN: 978-1-988066-75-2

Design and layout: Lindsay Maclachlan, White Walnut Design

Cover illustration courtesy of iStock Photo

Knowledge Champions

A special thank you to our Knowledge Champions for career development who helped to make possible the publication of the book.

Career Development Practitioners
Certification Board of Ontario

CDPCBO (Career Development Practitioners Certification Board of Ontario), is a not-for-profit organization supporting the growth of the Career Development profession in Ontario through certification, professional development, and advocacy. Nurturing Career Development Professionals strengthens the field of practice, increases competence and professionalism in the field, and provides quality assurance to clients, employers, and funders.
cdpcbo.org

CERIC

CERIC is a charitable organization that advances education and research in career development, in order to increase the economic and social well-being of people in Canada. It funds projects to develop innovative resources that build the knowledge and skills of diverse career professionals. CERIC also hosts Cannexus, Canada's largest career development conference, publishes the *Canadian Journal of Career Development*, and runs the CareerWise / OrientAction websites.
ceric.ca

Douglas College

Douglas College Continuing Education offers online training for Career Professionals to prepare them for the world of work at the start of their career, mid-career and as they move into management. We offer a foundational, an advanced and customized certificates in Career Development. We provide customized in-house training across Canada.
douglascollege.ca/FACS-ce

MAGNET

Magnet

Based at Toronto Metropolitan University (TMU), Magnet is Canada's only Digital Community Workforce System. Magnet connects labour market supply and demand to support the vision of an effective and well-coordinated employment and training system in partnership with a community of government, employment, industry, and enterprise organizations.

magnetnetwork.ca

nscda
N O V A   S C O T I A
Career Development Association

Nova Scotia Career Development Association

The Nova Scotia Career Development Association (NSCDA) is a not-for-profit professional organization with more than 800 members. The NSCDA provides training, certification and membership services to strengthen the career development profession within Nova Scotia and elsewhere and, ultimately, to positively impact employment and economic outcomes.

nscda.ca

UNIVERSITY OF CALGARY
CONTINUING EDUCATION

University of Calgary, Continuing Education

University of Calgary Continuing Education offers a wide range of seminars, courses and programs to individuals and organizations seeking opportunities for professional development and personal enrichment. Our online programs include a micro-credential in Career Development Professional Essentials, and certificates in Career Development & Academic Advising and Adult Learning specializing in Career & Academic Advising.

conted.ucalgary.ca/careerdev

Reviews for *Practice Principles: Career Theories and Models at Work*

This book is more than just a follow-up to *Career Theories and Models at Work: Ideas for Practice* (Arthur et al., 2019). Inside, you'll find eight essential principles that offer a framework for practitioners of career guidance, counseling, and consultation to metacognize their practice in a reflective and structured manner. These principles are equally beneficial for researchers seeking to connect their work with real-world applications. This exceptional book significantly elevates the quality of both practice and research. I extend my utmost respect to the authors.

- **Teruyuki Fujita, Professor, Career Education, Institute of Human Sciences, University of Tsukuba, Japan**

Simply brilliant! Most novel and creative way to bring one's own AI (authentic intelligence) into self-supervision of their practice. Only here are the eight principles jelled from 295 practices weaved from 43 chapters on the theory and models defining career development found. The "Career Practice Reflection Guide" magically injects a personal supervisor within your practice. This changed my practice. I'll never supervise without it again!

- **Rich Feller Ph.D, LPC, JCTC, Professor, Counseling and Career Development and University Distinguished Teaching Scholar, Colorado State University and Executive Director Career Development Network**

This is a treasure trove of career theories and practical examples, demonstrating their real-world applications. The authors invite readers on a captivating journey through a rich tapestry of ideas, strategies, and methods designed to create a profound deep understanding of how we can inspire and nurture individuals' curiosity and decision-making through career dialogue and exploration. Whether you are an experienced career practitioner or a novice in guidance and counselling, this book serves as a thought-provoking and introspective "how to guide," unlocking creativity, confidence, and competence in lifelong learning. It reminds us of the importance of both pedagogic wisdom and practice-based principles, values, and ethos to create effective models for personal development. I wholeheartedly recommend this work, as it underscores the importance of self-discovery and skillful practice, compelling you to take action.

- **Deirdre Hughes, Associate Professor, University of Warwick, Institute for Employment Research (IER) and Co-Founder of CareerChat UK Ltd.**

This book consolidates the complexities and addresses the practicalities of how to provide effective career development services in a most comprehensive manner. This is the first book I have read that deals with the core of career development services and what it is that career development practitioners should focus on to provide a valuable service. The five core practices for career practitioners offers a model to guide the work of practitioners in a way that will ensure an ethical and efficient service that is continually enhanced. I can confidently say that *Career Theories and Models at Work: Ideas for Practice*, and *Career Theories and Models at Work: Practice Principles* will become known as the two foundational resources for all career development practitioners with an interest in providing an effective career development service. I would like to thank the authors for sharing their wealth of knowledge and contributing to the career development profession through these assets.

- Christopher John Beukes, Chief Executive Officer, South African Career Development Association

This new book, *Practice Principles: Career Theories and Models* at Work, is an excellent tool that will support professional development and daily reflection among practitioners, both by themselves as well as together with colleagues. The book inspires to dig deeper into the different theories and models and to reflect upon them based on your own experience.

- Karin Asplund, President, The Swedish Association of Guidance Counsellors

The work of career professionals is critically important. The eight principles and practice points in this book will ground and support you in the complex challenges you face day-to-day. This is every career professional's go-to guide for theory-informed practice.

- Sareena Hopkins, Executive Director, Canadian Career Development Foundation (CCDF)

A must read for all career development professionals regardless of experience, *Practice Principles: Career Theories and Models* is the perfect accompaniment to *Career Theories and Models at Work: Ideas for Practice*. This informative new book will support anyone wanting to truly understand the career theory to practice interface while making sure they have laid the foundations for quality career development work.

- Heather Lowery-Kappes, National President, Career Development Association of New Zealand 2020-2023

This book bridges the divide between theory and practice, offering readers a comprehensive understanding of conceptualization and intervention. The well-crafted chapters explore a diverse array of topics, ensuring a thorough coverage of the subject matter. I wholeheartedly recommend this book to my students, confident that it will enrich their learning experience and enhance their practical skills.

- Zhi-Jin Hou, Professor, Faculty of Psychology, Beijing Normal University

Table of Contents

Preface

This book emanates from our second project with CERIC about the application of career theories and models in practice. Our first CERIC project emerged from our interest in helping career practitioners translate theory into practice. In developing the edited collection *Career Theories and Models at Work: Ideas for Practice* (Arthur et al., 2019)*, we emphasized the theory–practice link: **Career practice in contemporary times requires practitioners to be equipped with the latest developments in the field. This includes knowledge about current theories and models and strategies for applying that knowledge in their work with clients who seek career support**. We have advocated for strengthening the ethical foundations of career practice, through supporting practitioners to enhance their knowledge about theory and how theory informs practice. We have received wonderful feedback from practitioners in many countries who have read our first book and stated how much they have learned from a resource that was aimed at making theory more accessible and useful.

When we finished reviewing and editing the chapters of our first book, we began to discuss what we had learned. Each of the 43 chapters in *Career Theories and Models at Work: Ideas for Practice* focused on a specific theory or model and concluded with a list of practice points derived from the unique theory or model. We discussed the patterns that we noticed across the practice points of several chapters. As a result, we began to consider how a focus on the practice points could be leveraged to respond to practitioners' feedback for resources that they could apply in their everyday practices.

Our second CERIC-sponsored project is also aimed at supporting practitioners to strengthen their connections between practice and theory. We decided to emphasize the practice points and how they can be organized and synthesized to facilitate theory-informed career practice. This second project builds on the success of the first book by offering practitioners a "go-to" guide that helps them to learn more about ideas for practice, derived from theories and models.

Our second book offers a novel approach, through articulating core career practice principles. In determining the practice principles, we conducted a qualitative research analysis to synthesize the practice points into useful principles for everyday career practice. Through this process, the second book honours our commitment to strengthening theory–practice connections and demonstrating how practice can also inform theories and models. Although the practice principles seem relatively straightforward, they are always nuanced by the experiences of practitioners, the experiences and presenting issues of clients, and by practice contexts.

You can choose to use this second book as a resource on its own to learn about foundational principles of career development practice. In Chapter 1, we invite you to develop a personal vignette or case scenario that you will use as a basis for exploring and applying the practice principles discussed in subsequent chapters. The reflection prompts in Chapters 2–9 were designed to probe the topics and examples offered in each chapter. In Chapter 10, we consider the relationships between theory and practice, potential future innovations, applying your learning, and reflecting on your professional development needs. In Chapter 10, you will also find details about five core practices that we have derived from our synthesis of the practice principles. We also created a new tool for reflexive career practice; the *Career Practice Reflection Guide* in the Appendix is a compilation of the reflection questions and prompts from the previous chapters.

Further, if you would like to gain more in-depth knowledge about the origins of the principles and illustrative practice points, you can easily trace them back to the chapters on the specific theories and models in our first book, *Career Theories and Models at Work: Ideas for Practice*.

We hope that this book will inspire you to review and renew connections between theory and practice. We look forward to learning from you about the ways that you have applied the principles to strengthen theory-informed practice.

- Nancy, Roberta, and Mary

*Citations attributed to Roberta Neault, including *Career Theories and Models at Work: Ideas for Practice*, were written by the second editor of this book, Roberta Borgen, whose name changed in 2020 with her marriage.

Acknowledgement

Funding was provided through a Learning and Professional Development Project grant from CERIC.

Dedication

We dedicate this book to the authors of career theories and models and to practitioners whose perspectives have contributed to innovative theory-practice connections in the field of career development.

Chapter 1

Strengthening Career Theory–Practice Connections

This chapter provides the background to our book projects that have focused on assisting career practitioners to use theory-based practice. The focus of Chapter 1 is to:

- Consider the nature of career development theory and its relationship to practice
- Consider how theory can strengthen professionalism
- Describe how we distilled the eight practice principles on which the next eight chapters are based
- Introduce the practice principles
- Prompt you to develop a personal vignette that you will use to reflect on the application of the practice principles

Background

In our edited book, *Career Theories and Models at Work: Ideas for Practice* (Arthur et al., 2019), the authors of each of the 43 chapters overviewed a theory or model of career development, demonstrated its application in a case study, and provided practice points that could guide that application. This book, *Practice Principles: Career Theories and Models at Work*, is informed by those practice points. What we observed about the chapters and practice points is a relationship between the theories and models; models may be the origins on which theories are developed or they may be derived from one or more theories. This book is informed by the practice points related to the theories and models and builds on that work by synthesizing the practice points into eight practice principles, with the specific aim of assisting career practitioners to strengthen career theory–practice connections. To achieve this aim, each of the following eight chapters focuses specifically on one practice principle. We invite you at the end of this chapter to develop a case vignette to use for reflection on the practice principles described in the chapters that follow.

We begin the first chapter in this book by considering what theory is, how it informs career practice, and the role it plays in professional standards for career practitioners. We then explain the relationship between this book and its parent book, *Career Theories and Models at Work: Ideas for Practice* (Arthur et al., 2019). Next, we explain how we synthesized the practice points from that book to arrive at the eight practice principles which form the basis of the subsequent chapters in this book. We conclude this book with a chapter that considers the implications of theory-informed practice. In this concluding chapter we draw connections between the eight practice principles to identify five core practices for career practitioners. Our book also includes a Career Practice Reflection Guide that we hope will encourage you to continually reflect on your practice and to participate in ongoing professional learning about theory–practice connections.

What Is Theory and How Does It Inform Career Practice?

Theory is essentially an explanation of a particular phenomenon (Lent, 2017). In the case of this book, the phenomenon is career development, which we know from our personal experience is complex, dynamic, and markedly influenced by contexts and cultures. The metaphor of "witness accounts" (McMahon, 2019a) has been used to describe the differing perspectives from which career development can be viewed and explained in detail. Theories can help us to "understand and describe people's career development and work experiences" (Ali & Brown, 2017, p. 73) and can "guide us in making sense of complex sets of information about how humans behave to help us understand them and to predict their behaviour in the future" (Swanson & Fouad, 2015, p. 12).

So how does career theory inform career practice? Career theory explains career decision-making, the process of career development, and how these are influenced by contexts and cultures (McMahon, 2019a). Theory underpins career assessment and can guide us in case conceptualization (McMahon, 2019a). Importantly, an understanding of career theory is essential for professionalization of the discipline of career development (McMahon, 2019a). In this chapter we examine what these core ideas about theory mean for you and your practice.

Assisting people with their *career decision-making* was the fundamental reason for the emergence of the field of career development when it was known as vocational guidance. Today, career decision-making remains the primary reason for the work of career practitioners, who assist people with their decisions about transition into learning and work, transition through work, and transition from work to retirement. Some theories help us to understand how career decisions are made (e.g., Holland, 1997; Lent & Brown, 2021; Osborn, Dozier, Bullock Yowell et al., 2019; Osborn, Dozier, Peterson et al., 2019; Parsons, 1909).

Career development is widely understood as a *developmental process* across the lifespan, beginning in early childhood and continuing into older age. Some theories (e.g., Gottfredson, 2005; Super, 1990) help us to understand career development stages that people pass through, across their lifespans. These theories help us to think about age- or stage-appropriate tasks in our career development work. These theories have also contributed to conceptualizing the blueprint frameworks that have been developed in several countries to guide the work of career practitioners (e.g., *Australian Blueprint for Career Development* [Commonwealth of Australia, 2022]; *Pan-Canadian Competency Framework for Career Development Professionals* [Canadian Career Development Foundation, 2021a]). These frameworks identify age- or stage-appropriate competencies that can be developed by clients in career education, career programs, and career counselling.

Since the days of Parsons (1909), *career assessment* has been ever-present in career development work. Career assessment instruments, such as surveys and questionnaires, are regularly used by career practitioners to help clients learn more about themselves. These instruments assess personal attributes such as interests, values, or personality and produce quantitative data. Some qualitative career assessment instruments, such as card sorts and mind maps, are guided processes that help people to tell their career stories.

Case conceptualization refers to how practitioners organize and make sense of the considerable information clients present, with a view to planning a course of action with the client. Career theories offer practitioners a range of perspectives through which to consider case conceptualization and may suggest potential interventions.

Everyone's career development occurs in *contexts and cultures*. These have implications for the presenting issues that clients bring to career practitioners and for the way in which those practitioners work with clients with diverse worldviews and life experiences. Some career theories and models provide insight into the influences of contexts and cultures and offer ideas about potential interventions.

Every profession has a body of theory that underpins it and sets it apart from other professions. The body of theory underpinning career development dates back more than a century, and in that time many career theories have been developed. Career development theory distinguishes our profession from other professions and provides a foundation for practice. Understanding and knowing how to apply relevant theory is a hallmark of *professionalism*.

Theory as a Core Competency in Professional Standards and Guidelines

Professionalism is the reason that knowledge about career theory and the ability to apply it have been included in professional standards and guidelines for career practitioners in many countries, including Canada and Australia. For example, the International Association for Educational and Vocational Guidance (2018) included the following core competency in its *International Competencies for Educational and Vocational Guidance Practitioners*: "Integrate theory and research into practice in guidance, career development, counselling, and consultation." The *Professional Standards for Australian Career Development Practitioners* incorporated career development theory as a core competency which can be demonstrated by describing and applying in practice "major career development theories, concepts, research, and associated models and frameworks" (Career Industry Council of Australia, 2019, p. 11). Similarly, the *Pan-Canadian Competency Framework for Career Development Professionals* included "understand career development theories and models" and "apply career development theories and models" as foundational knowledge that distinguishes career development from other fields (Canadian Career Development Foundation, 2021a). Clearly then, the application of career theory is central to professional practice in career development. Theory though, is not static; theories evolve and new theories emerge. Theories from the past continue to inform our current perspectives and practice, and contemporary theories add new perspectives to our understanding of career development. Keeping up-to-date with the latest developments in career theory is a requirement of professional standards and guidelines and a responsibility of career practitioners.

Theory-Informed Practice Principles

Knowing how to apply career theory can sometimes be challenging for practitioners. Our edited book *Career Theories and Models at Work: Ideas for Practice* (Arthur et al., 2019) provided an overview of 43 different theories and models—one per chapter. We invited the chapter authors to explain their theory or model, demonstrate its application in a case study, and provide a list of practice points for practitioners. The practice points identified the key ideas that would assist practitioners to use the theory or model. In total, across the 43 chapters, 295 practice points were listed. As we read and re-read the practice points, we noticed patterns and similarities across chapters in the ideas that the authors deemed central to career practice. This sparked our curiosity: Could it be possible to distil some key principles about career development practice irrespective of theory? After much discussion, we planned a way forward. The result is the eight practice principles on which this book is based.

How We Developed the Practice Principles

So, how did we synthesize 295 practice points into eight practice principles? We started with a list of the practice points which became our data source, or the base of information that we used to inform the practice principles. We employed a qualitative research analysis process and independently considered and coded the practice points according to the main idea in each one. This was the first step in our synthesis of the practice points. Although the three of us assigned many similar codes, some of our initial codes revealed our different impressions and understandings. These differences were instructive and the subject of many discussions through which we were able to reach consensus on the codes. To further refine our analysis and move us closer to our goal of identifying key practice principles, we looked for similarities and differences between the codes and were able to identify eight groups. We again reviewed the codes within each group to determine an overarching name for the group that would be representative of the content as a practice principle; the codes within each group were themselves subdivided and form subordinate topics of each practice principle.

The result of this analysis process is the following eight practice principles:

1. Career development practice integrates practitioner reflection.
2. Career development practice is built on relationships.
3. Career development practice involves collaboration with clients.
4. Career development practice requires customization.
5. Career development practice is based on theory.
6. Career development practice occurs in cultural contexts.
7. Career development practice incorporates social justice advocacy.
8. Career development practice involves collaboration with other professionals.

Each of the next eight chapters focuses on one of these practice principles. The topics relevant to each practice principle are identified and explained in the chapters and illustrated by quotes from the practice points. You will notice that practice points from the same authors are used in more than one chapter. This is because the topics within and across practice principles are related and illustrate that practice needs to be integrated.

The concluding chapter revisits the theory–practice connections outlined in this chapter and encourages you to reflect on what you have learned, on potential innovations in your practice, and on your professional development learning needs. We hope that you enjoy reading about the practice principles and considering how can you embed them in your current practice. Additionally, we invite you to consider how the chapter content based on each practice principle might help you to identify topics for continued professional learning.

Making the Most of This Book: A Vignette for Reflection

The goal of this book is to help you apply theories and models in practice. To get the most out of your reading about the practice principles and their associated topics, we encourage you to reflect on the content of each chapter by applying it to a case vignette. Rather than providing you with a fictitious vignette, we want to emphasize the personal nature of learning, and so we invite you to reflect instead on experiences in your own life or career practice. It is time now to develop your own case vignette—one that you will revisit at the end of each chapter.

To develop your vignette, think about the practice scenarios you have worked on or are presently working on in your current work context. Let those scenarios roll through your mind until one seems more prominent for you than the others. Give that case a name. If your current practice does not involve engaging with clients, reflect on your own career development until a particular scenario stands out for you. Give that scenario a name.

Under the name of your vignette, record important information in point form. The following questions may guide you. If you are using a scenario from your own life and career, you may adapt the questions to suit your circumstances. Record your answers so that you have them on hand when you reach the end of the subsequent chapters.

- What was the presenting issue?
- What did the client want from you?
- What was your initial response to this issue?
- What were the goals you set with the client?
- What was the cultural context of the client?
- What factors from the client's context have you considered, or might you need to consider?
- What is your own cultural context?
- What skills/techniques/interventions worked well with this client?
- What skills/techniques/interventions did not go so well?
- What theory or model was informing your practice?
- What was your relationship like with the client?
- What were key points in your work with this client?
- What were the outcomes of your work with this client?

We encourage you to use this vignette to reflect on the content after reading each chapter, using the prompts and questions provided at the end of the chapter. The prompts and questions are all collated in Appendix 1.

Conclusion

In writing this book, we advocate for theory-informed practice. Building on a base of practice points elicited from the 43 theories and models presented by chapter authors in the book *Career Theories and Models at Work: Ideas for Practice* (Arthur et al., 2019), we now offer a set of principles that can be used in everyday practice. In presenting these practice principles, we have intentionally highlighted the contributions of the chapter authors by citing their practice points to illustrate the topics in the chapter authors' own words. We hope that, as you work through the following chapters, you will take time to reflect on your own careers and practice roles as well as the application of the principles contained in this book.

Chapter 2

Career Development Practice Integrates Practitioner Reflection

This chapter orients readers to reflection as fundamental for professional practice and continuous learning. The focus of Chapter 2 is to:

- Position reflection as a foundation for professional practice
- Invite you to reflect on your personal journey of career development
- Examine how your personal values, beliefs, and life experiences influence your professional roles
- Consider the relationships between reflection and practice
- Provide examples of theory-based reflection practices

As you read, pause periodically to reflect on the personal vignette that you created in Chapter 1. Questions for further reflection are listed at the end of the chapter.

Reflective Practice Is a Foundation for Career Practice

Reflective practice is generally considered to be a requirement of professionals in many disciplines, such as teaching and counselling, and it is a cornerstone for professionals working in the career development sector and career industry (Neary & Johnson, 2016). The reason is that reflective practice helps practitioners to consider the skills and knowledge required for their roles, to identify *what works*, and to identify areas for future learning. In this chapter, we explain the *why* of reflective practice, introduce the *what* and some topics for reflection, and share the *how*— suggested strategies for ongoing reflection. Although there are many models and definitions of reflection, two aspects are typically emphasized for professional practice (Bassot, 2014). First, using the metaphor of a mirror, reflection encourages self-observation to achieve a level of self-awareness. This includes how our personal experiences and socialization have shaped our values and beliefs and how we view the world around us. In other words, reflection about our worldviews helps us to understand the lens through which we view other people, including their vocational and career-related behaviour (Arthur, 2019a). Second, reflection involves a process or approach that helps us to be thoughtful practitioners (Bassot, 2014).

This process involves being intentional about the application of career theories and models to determine *what is working, what is not working, and what could be done differently*. Reflection can help you to facilitate change, through thinking about your work in new ways and using that information to creatively apply career theories and models in practice.

There is a long history of models of reflection designed for professionals, dating from the seminal work of Kolb (1984). In a four-step process, professionals were encouraged to (a) identify an actual practice experience, (b) reflect on the experience, (c) gain new insights and knowledge, and (d) test out new knowledge through active experimentation. Many scholars have expanded and revised the original model to strengthen the process of ongoing professional learning (see Bassot, 2014, 2016), and to incorporate both cognitive and affective domains of experience, (e.g., *What do you think about your practice? How do you feel about your practice?*).

Schön (1992) emphasized two modes of reflection to guide practitioners. The first mode, reflection-in-action, is to think about ways to improve practice in the moment—to critically evaluate what is happening in the actual or in vivo time frame and to respond by shifting or reframing your application of practice knowledge. The second mode, reflection-on-action, occurs after the live practice situation. The orientation in the second mode is generally intended to improve future practice. A hybrid approach has been suggested as a third mode: reflection-on-self-in/on-action involves building conscious personal awareness during practice sessions and during the review of practice sessions (Collins et al., 2010).

One of the trends in the literature on professional reflection emphasizes an active approach to critical reflexivity. This means being willing and able to review your practice as a critical observer, to reflect on actions taken, to reflect on areas of strength and areas for improvement, and to identify areas for learning (Bassot, 2016; Collins et al., 2010). Reflection is not a linear process; rather, it is reflexive process, in which learning occurs in a cyclical fashion, as new knowledge builds on prior knowledge, new ideas are tested and new approaches are tried, and new discoveries are integrated into practice. The critically reflexive practitioner engages in a continuous loop of building on and revisiting foundational knowledge to deepen understanding and to enhance the application of career theories and models in practice.

Reflection on Self and Career: Start Here!

Many approaches to reflection in professional practice focus on the interaction between practitioners and their clients. Reflection about the working alliance is certainly an important aspect of our professional work, and we encourage you to connect the content in this chapter with the content in Chapters 3 and 4. However, we suggest that there is some preliminary work to be completed before emphasizing reflection about other people. We urge you to first reflect on your personal experiences and how these have shaped your understandings about career-related behaviour.

Self-awareness is generally considered to be an essential competency for professional practice. In other words, "reflect on your worldview. The ways that career practitioners were socialized and educated influence their views of careers, jobs, and occupational success" (Arthur, 2019b, p. 30). Reflection can help you to gain insights about how your worldview shapes your professional roles and about the many influences on your own career and the careers of the clients you serve. "Our careers are the product of a myriad

> **Reflect on your own systems of influences and on your practice.** *Be aware of your own system of influences and how they impact you in career counselling (e.g., in your approach to counselling, your attitude to clients, the values you hold).* (McMahon & Patton, 2019, p. 247)

of changing influences all interacting with each other. Beginning to understand and scope these influences is a good starting point in understanding our strengths, weaknesses, opportunities, and limitations" (Pryor & Bright, 2019b, p. 357). Your experiences and clients' experiences may seem similar, but no two people have identical influences on their careers. Some people have many resources to support their career development and other people have faced many barriers or social inequities, a point that we expand upon in Chapter 8.

> **Self-reflection.** *To what extent has your career progression to date been influenced by your social and economic background? What barriers have you overcome at career turning points and who/what have been the key influences on your career decisions? How important has community been for you?* (Bimrose, 2019b, p. 62)

Our worldviews are shaped, over time, through our relationships. Therefore, it is important to "reflect on the relationships in your life. Become aware of how your own career choices have been influenced by important others and vice versa" (Popadiuk, 2019, p. 336). It is through our personal relationships that our values and beliefs are formed.

Values are part of our personal repertoire; values are embedded in our professional roles. Therefore, it is important to "notice your values. Many models of career counselling value independence and autonomy; [Relational-Cultural Theory] honours the interdependence of people's lives" (Popadiuk, 2019, p. 336). You want to "acknowledge that your values might be different than those held by your clients and strive to be client-centred in your approach to career counselling" (Arthur, 2019b, p. 30). We must focus on what our clients deem to be important.

Reflecting on your values and beliefs will enable you to recognize that there will be times when you are faced with values conflicts and to prepare for challenges to your personal worldviews. Gaining personal awareness is a starting point to "take responsibility for your own biases and prejudices" (Pope, 2019, p. 346), and to avoid imposing your beliefs and values in professional relationships. Your life experiences, key relationships, and career trajectories will contain patterns that are similar and different to the life experiences of the clients you serve. "We must resist the temptation to 'fix' the person or their problem, rather than encourage them to see their careers in terms of flow and counselling in terms of developing and enhancing strategies and perspectives to negotiate chaos" (Pryor & Bright, 2019a, p. 357). In other words, as career practitioners, we need to be prepared to work within the contexts of our clients' lives.

To summarize, we advocate for personal reflection about how your life experiences shape your views about career-related behaviour, the kinds of interventions that might be applied, and preferred outcomes (Arthur, 2019a). Personal experiences shape how we understand key concepts such as work, careers, the status of jobs, career planning and decision-making, and associated concepts such as career progression and success. You might also "reflect on the chance events that have happened in your own/a client's career" (Pryor & Bright, 2019a, p. 357) and reflect on what led you to evaluate those events as negative or positive, limiting or enhancing your options. These are some examples to anchor your personal exploration of career development. To reiterate, self-reflection involves gaining insights about your past and current experiences and how these personal experiences influence your role as a career development practitioner.

Reflection on Practice

In this chapter, we also want to set the stage for reflecting on practice. Earlier in this chapter, we introduced two approaches, reflecting as practice happens and reflecting on practice in retrospect, both of which emphasize the reflection process as ongoing professional learning. In subsequent chapters, we will emphasize in more detail some of the practice points from authors of career theories and models and provide more examples and possibilities to guide your reflection on practice. The selected examples in this chapter are intended to familiarize you with ways to integrate your personal reflections into your practice contexts.

Have you reflected on which theories and models guide your work? Do you use one main theory or model or more than one? Are you open to exploring different ways of approaching your practice? We remind readers that the work in this book was informed by the 43 different theories and models discussed in *Theories* and *Models at Work: Ideas for Practice* (Arthur et al., 2019). From the numerous theories and models available, you might choose to explore one or more that are unfamiliar to you and examine new practice applications. You might be more intentional in your choices and "select from the vocational literature those theories and bodies of research that are most useful to you" (Richardson, 2019, p. 368), to better understand a key concept and/or application in practice. For example, if you were working with a client who wished to explore how their skills might transfer from unpaid to paid work, it would be useful to select resources that help to explain how unpaid work is connected to social structures and to the gender-role strain that occurs for many clients. "The vocational literature has many theories and bodies of research that can guide you in facilitating the market [paid] work trajectories of clients" (Richardson, 2019, p. 368).

As a base of knowledge, theories and models can be used to help you reflect on clients and their contexts and to identify important influences on their career development. For example, when reflecting on a client's behaviour, you might "highlight aspects of adjustment styles that may be impeding an individual's ability to seek change in their work environment (e.g., assertiveness)" (Woodend, 2019, p. 462). However, understanding a client's presenting issues and viable interventions often extends beyond the individual. "Systemic influences can be powerful. Help clients to view their concerns within larger systems influences to avoid internalizing blame and to address barriers" (Arthur, 2019b, p. 30). Examining the influences on clients' presenting concerns not only exposes potential barriers related to their career issues but also affords exploration of strengths, patterns of behaviour, and/or relationships that may be relevant for designing effective interventions.

Remember that people's lives are situated within local, national, and international contexts. The significance and meanings of those contexts will be nuanced by peoples' experiences, over time and across situations, and by the cultural beliefs and values that are embedded in people's worldviews. Therefore, you are encouraged to "reflect about culture in everyday practice with all clients" (Arthur, 2019b, p. 30). Exploration of contexts and cultural influences can be useful for designing client-centred, collaborative approaches to assessment and interventions, further discussed in Chapters 3, 4, and 5.

To recap, we encourage you to reflect on the cultural contexts of your own life and those of your clients, to appreciate similarities and/or differences in

> *Career counsellors must fine-tune their ability to pinpoint the origin of these shifts [in perspective]—which are delicate, fragile, and intangible—in their clients' perception of the world of work.* They will then be better able to help their clients in their continuous career transitions. (Riverin-Simard & Simard, 2019, p. 377)

worldviews, and to keep the focus on your clients' experiences. These key points are elaborated in Chapter 7.

> **Be curious.** What makes this client tick? Be in the moment with the client, and follow your curiosity. Your questions, requests for clarification, prompts to dig deeper, and reflections of meaning are ways to learn more about the client's experiences and motivations. (Brott, 2019, p. 82)

Career development practitioners are inevitably involved in interpersonal interactions when they work with clients. Therefore, it is important to reflect on how you can build effective relationships and how you can strategically work in collaboration with clients to support their goals for change. As you reflect on relationships, "consider the nature of your relationships with your clients. How are you helping your clients feel that they really matter? What concrete steps are you taking to pass this message along?" (Amundson, 2019, p. 9). For example, practising intercultural communication demonstrates empathy. When clients feel understood, within the contexts of their lives, they are more likely to engage in interventions (Dionne & Dupuis, 2019).

The content in this chapter is intended to orient you to the importance of self-reflection and reflection about practice, as avenues to learn and apply new knowledge. "Envision your role and actions. Visualize what you wish your practice to be and the particular ways to contribute to the mission of your employer" (Viviers, 2019, p. 431). This latter point adds another dimension to reflection: considering organizational influences. Career development practice occurs within the context of employment settings, funding mandates, and the norms of organizations where career services are delivered. Reflection can help to link practice to organizational goals, ideally improving organizational practices while also improving service delivery for clients.

> **Pause.** Take some time to step back and examine what is happening in the work you are doing. Are you making adjustments to fit with the needs of your clients or just following a traditional framework? Does your counselling space look like a creative space where collaborative work is being done? (Amundson, 2019, p. 9)

In summary, reflection helps career development practitioners to be more intentional in their practices through the pathways of learning about themselves, their clients, and the application of knowledge in the settings where they deliver services. "Reflect on your learning from clients. Use your learning to identify areas for growth and be intentional about seeking resources and professional development" (Arthur, 2019b, p. 30). It is through the relational processes of career practice that we can test out new ideas and integrate new practice knowledge into the organizational and employment contexts where career services are provided.

Reflection Models and Tools to Support You

As a starting point, we invite you to explore different approaches to reflection. You might find it helpful to apply different approaches to an actual case scenario, such as the one you identified at the end of Chapter 1. This process can help you to select your preferred approach or combine ideas from various sources to create a hybrid approach to guide your reflection process (Dressler et al., 2018). You might also work with a colleague or two to try out different reflection models, such as the ones described earlier in the chapter. After each person selects a different model and works through the reflection process, you could share your respective impressions about the models, including what was useful and any limitations. These suggestions are intended to help you select and customize your reflection process.

You might also enjoy exploring other types of tools that have been developed to aid reflective practice. Some examples include writing techniques such as journalling and creative writing. Remember, "you don't have to be a counsellor or published author to facilitate career writing. Get some training and play. There are articles, exercises, and courses available to learn the method" (Lengelle et al., 2019, p. 193). There are also questionnaires designed with prompts to guide reflection (Arthur, 2017; Neary & Johnson, 2016). Such tools and reflection processes are not intended to be time-consuming or overtaxing. Incorporating reflection into your everyday practice can help you to anchor your work amidst the many demands of professional practice. "In carrying out your work, do you find yourself overwhelmed with all the actions that need to be taken? Do you take time to step back from the busyness and listen to that small inner voice that is trying to be heard?" (Amundson, 2019, p. 9). Taking a little time each day for reflection can help you to feel engaged with your work and empowered about your professional knowledge and applications in practice. Furthermore, engaging with reflection may help you to become more aware of the challenges and rewards of skill development as well as techniques to perhaps suggest to clients and encourage them to practice. Through your own

> **Practice what you preach.** *For the counsellor, it is necessary to know the core processes from personal experience. Practising them (e.g., mindful listening) has positive effects on the counsellor's own psychological health, attitude, and competence. (Luken & de Folter, 2019, p. 205)*

experience and personal awareness, you might gain insights you can share to promote client change.

Newer and experienced career practitioners are encouraged to engage in supervision as an ongoing process to enhance their professional learning (McMahon & Patton, 2000; Patton & McMahon, 2021). This chapter has emphasized individual reflection through self-supervision to facilitate reflexivity about career practice (McIlveen & Patton, 2010). Reflection can also be peer-supervised, integrated into formal supervision and case consultation with colleagues. Whether you engage in individual processes or in shared processes with a supervisor or colleagues, there are many ways to integrate reflection into practice. Lastly, we have provided reflection questions at the end of this and subsequent chapters to help you apply the key ideas in your practice context!

Conclusion

The focus of this chapter was on the guiding principle that career development practice integrates practitioner reflection. We encourage you to reflect on your personal journey of career development and the many influences that have shaped your understanding of the world of work and career-related behaviour. Your personal reflection sets the stage for understanding how your beliefs and values influence your professional roles. We encourage you to access the models and tools that have been designed to help you incorporate reflection as an ongoing learning process in your professional learning and development.

Career Development Practice Integrates Practitioner Reflection: Reflection Questions

Revisit the personal vignette you created in Chapter 1. Use the following questions to apply the content of this chapter to your vignette.

1. What experiences have been key influences in your personal career development?
2. How did gender influence your pursuit of occupations or the occupations your family members pursued and selected?
3. Which aspects of your identity other than gender (e.g., ethnicity, social class, religion, ability), or their intersections, influence your pursuit of occupations?
4. What were the views of your family and friends on issues such as the types of jobs considered desirable, unemployment, and career success? How did their views influence you?
5. How do you engage in reflective practice currently?
6. In what ways could you strengthen your engagement with reflective practice?

Chapter 3

Career Development Practice Is Built on Relationships

Building quality relationships is central to career development practice. The focus of Chapter 3 is to:

- Discuss the nature of practitioner–client relationships in career development practice
- Consider the practitioner–client relationship as a foundation for building an effective working alliance
- Provide examples of how to build effective relationships in career development practice

As you read, pause periodically to reflect on the personal vignette that you created in Chapter 1. Questions for further reflection are listed at the end of each chapter.

Building Quality Career Development Practitioner-Client Relationships

Career development practice is based on relationships between practitioners and clients. In such relationships, the qualities of mutual respect and trust (Corey, 2019), acceptance, understanding, and caring are critical. According to Rogers (1951), a preeminent figure in the field of counselling, the quality of the client–counsellor relationship is essential for promoting client growth. Rogers proposed three core conditions he believed would facilitate a climate of growth for clients: (a) congruence, (b) unconditional positive regard, and (c) empathy. Congruence refers to the counsellor being genuine; unconditional positive regard is about demonstrating acceptance of, and care for, clients; and empathy is about trying to see the world through the eyes of the other person. To build a quality client-counsellor relationship, you must "practice your empathy skills. Place yourself into the client's shoes" (Spangar, 2019, p. 400).

Although Rogers's work was in the field of counselling, similar views about the practitioner–client relationship have been expressed in career counselling. For example, Amundson (2018) discussed the importance of creating a mattering climate where clients feel respected and feel that they have the undivided attention of the practitioner. It is important that clients feel that the career practitioner genuinely cares about them. Essential to the relationship is the practitioner's ability to understand the "experiential world" (Corey, 2019, p. 20) of the client and to be able to demonstrate this to the client. Both client and practitioner have a role in co-creating the client–practitioner relationship (Corey, 2019). The relationship between practitioners and clients has been described as a working partnership in which negotiation between, and participation of, both client and career practitioner are essential (Peavy, 2004).

The relationship between career practitioners and clients is sometimes referred to as the working alliance which basically refers to the client and practitioner "working together to achieve agreed goals" (Corey, 2019, p. 20). There is agreement in the literature that the working alliance increases over the course of career counselling, and there seems to be a relationship between the working alliance and the outcomes of the session although only a small number of studies have examined this (Whiston et al., 2016). The working alliance is widely considered to comprised three elements: (a) goals, (b) tasks, and (c) bonds (Bordin, 1979). Goals are negotiated between clients and practitioners, tasks are the processes engaged in by clients and practitioners to achieve the goals, and bonds refer to the relationship between clients and practitioners (Whiston et al., 2016). The working alliance is affected by a range of factors including client factors, practitioner factors, and intervention strategies.

Every client is different, and so building a working alliance cannot be formulaic; it needs to be individualized for each client and a one-size-fits-all approach will not work (Corey, 2019). The goals negotiated between clients and practitioners influence the tasks selected. Goal-setting may be twofold: first, setting an overall goal for the career counselling; and second, setting goals for each session. Goals need to be revisited periodically and practitioners need to be flexible enough to be able to adjust the strategies and processes they use, checking in with clients to ensure that the overall goals are met. Clients need to be actively involved in the process of developing the working alliance (Corey, 2019).

Clients and career practitioners are cultural beings (Arthur, 2019a). Each has a complex cultural identity founded in elements such as gender, nationality, ethnic background, and religion. Culture may influence attitudes to help-seeking, as well as the strategies, techniques and assessments used and as the type of actions possible (Evans & Sejuit, 2021). Career practitioners need to be aware of their own cultural background and how it influences their work and "[g]uard against stereotypes" (Arthur, 2019b, p. 30). The influence of culture and context on career practice is discussed in detail in Chapter 7.

Creating a Safe Space

Clients who seek assistance from career practitioners may be doing so for the first time and may know little to nothing about how career counselling works. In addition, they are sharing their concerns with a person they may never have met before and therefore, may experience some vulnerability. Creating a safe space in which clients feel able to share their concerns, thoughts, emotions, and feelings is at the heart of the client–practitioner relationship. A good starting point for creating a safe space is to "hear the client's story. This is a critical first step regardless of theoretical approach" (Magnusson & Redekopp, 2019, p. 216).

Safe spaces are built on trust. "Establish an effective working alliance. As in all types of counselling, it is important to build an effective relationship, through active listening, observation, and individualized responses" (Neault & Pickerell, 2019, p. 281). To create a safe space, it is important to "practice your empathy skills" (Spangar, 2019, p. 400) and to "practice your listening skills" (Spangar, 2019, p. 400). "As a rule of thumb, the counsellors should use about thirty per cent of the time speaking and the rest of the time in a listening mode" (Peavy, 2004, p. 62). In addition, practitioners need to use language that clients understand rather than the jargon of the discipline. Ensure that your office space is welcoming and that you "maintain a supportive atmosphere in your office" (Pope, 2019, p. 346).

> **Establish a respectful, caring, trusting, and mattering relationship with clients.** *Seeking help, in general from someone they don't know, may expose individuals to a sense of vulnerability. Relationship building is not a single step but is essential to work on throughout the counselling process.* (McMahon & Patton, 2019, p. 247).

Some career practice is conducted as a group intervention, and it is just as important to create a safe space in group settings as it is in one-to-one practice. Group interventions are typically organized when individuals share a common interest or concern, and support can be provided by the career practitioner as well as other group members. In groups, it is useful to "promote the sharing of stories. Help clients narrate and share their career-life stories with you, the career practitioner, but also with "others" in safe psychological spaces, especially when counselling is done in group contexts" (Maree, 2019, p. 226). It is incumbent on career practitioners working in group settings to consider the following points:

> Make it safe for students/clients to feel and express thoughts and emo-
> tions. Creative introductions where people aren't asked about their
> career or social standing make for inspiring starts to the process. A safe-
> enough space in which to work together is a matter of setting some
> guidelines, but more importantly a result of how grounded and relaxed
> you are in your own body. (Lengelle et al., 2019, p. 193)

This basically means, from Rogers's (1951) perspective, being genuine.

The more clients tell us and the more we can find out, the better positioned
we are to develop action plans with clients that are actionable and achievable
(Gergen & Gergen, 2006). If we don't take time to listen to client stories and gather as much information as possible, mismatches could occur in terms of the goal set in the working alliance or the strategies and processes we use, which in turn could lead to client disengagement. The importance of listening and information gathering cannot be understated and is core to assessment practices.

Encourage clients to speak openly about past experiences, thoughts, feelings, and contexts. This exploration serves to identify activity pathways. (Vondracek & Ford, 2019, p. 441)

Assessment Practices

Career assessment has been a feature of career practice since the inception of the discipline of vocational guidance which subsequently evolved into the discipline we now know as career development. Parsons (1909) developed one of the earliest career assessment instruments in the form of his "personal record and self-analysis" (Parsons, 1909, p. 27) questionnaire which contained over 100 questions to be completed by clients prior to their career counselling interview. What is significant about Parsons's career assessment instrument is the responsibility it placed on the client to be active and involved in the career counselling process (then known as vocational guidance).

The purpose of career assessment is to assist clients with career planning and decision making; essentially, career assessment helps clients to learn about themselves in a meaningful way, and helps career practitioners to build a holistic understanding of clients, their life histories, and their issues. Career assessment instruments may be qualitative or quantitative, formal or informal in nature (Watson & McMahon, 2015). Quantitative career assessments tend to be standardized, objective, and statistical, whereas qualitative career assessment instruments tend to be more open-ended, flexible, and non-statistical (McMahon, 2019b). Regardless of the instrument selected, "the needs of the client should be the primary driving force in selecting assessment techniques, and not the preferences and prejudices of the counsellor" (de Bruin & de Bruin, 2017, p. 186).

Just as creating a safe place and building an effective client–practitioner relationship are ongoing processes, so too is assessment. In fact, informal career assessment undertaken by clients is likely to be a reason that they seek the advice of a career practitioner. For example, clients may have reflected on their life, education, and employment and discovered something that has led them to seek career services. Career assessment comes in many forms and career practitioners may have a favourite instrument that they like to use. However, every client is unique and brings a new set of concerns to career counselling. Caution needs to be exercised about "one-size-fits-all" approaches as the uniqueness of clients warrants customization of practice, a topic explored in Chapter 5.

> *Ongoing assessment.*
> *All career development interventions must be based on an initial and ongoing assessment of an individual's personal resources, psychological functioning, and life conditions.*
> (Cournoyer & Lachance, 2019, p. 101)

> *Use stories and scores.* The use of both qualitative and quantitative instruments ensures that practice is based on a theoretically sound and practically viable strategy and conceptual framework, and meets the career-counselling needs of clients who experience meaning- and purpose-related challenges.
> (Maree, 2019, p. 226)

Whether to use a career instrument depends on the client and whether they think it might be useful to them. Engaging in career assessment in a way that maintains the client–counsellor relationship means explaining the assessment instrument to the client and why you think it might be useful to them and seeking their agreement to use it. This process recognizes that clients are experts in their lives and have an active role in determining the nature of the career services offered to them. Simply using a career assessment instrument because you like it without discussing its use with the client and without their consent may harm the client–counsellor relationship by devaluing the role of the client and elevating the practitioner into a more directive role. Career practitioners need to "be aware of the special issues when using career assessment inventories with individuals from various cultural communities" (Pope, 2019, p. 346). From the cultural preparedness viewpoint, the cultural appropriateness of career assessment instruments is an essential consideration; "it is important to evaluate the cultural relevance of methods and tools used in career guidance when working with students to match their needs and abilities" (Aravind & Arulmani, 2019, p. 19).

Goal Setting and Decision Making

Goal setting and decision making are essential parts of career practice. In fact, according to Bordin (1979), goals are central to the working alliance. Goal setting is a collaborative process based on the needs clients initially bring to career counselling. In counselling, goals provide a sense of direction (Corey, 2019); goal setting is guided by two questions: "'What outcomes do I want?' and 'What do I have to do to get them?'" (Egan, 2019, p. 309). In career practice, an essential early step is to "arrive at shared goals. Agree on what is to be accomplished through counselling" (Vondracek & Ford, 2019, p. 441). Thus, from the earliest stage of a client–practitioner relationship, an essential task is to "explore and clarify potential goals (educational or vocational/career)" (Vondracek & Ford, 2019, p. 441). Remember, client goals are influenced by cultural context (Corey, 2019).

Setting goals helps clients to focus their attention, direct their effort and energy, and search for strategies (Egan, 2019); "clear and specific goals help clients persist" (Egan, 2019, p. 310) and provide a sense of direction for the collaborative work of clients and practitioners. SMART goals are Specific, Measurable, Achievable, Relevant, and Timely. Setting goals gives clients hope because it offers them a way to move forward. It is possible, however, for goals to be revised and for new goals to be set "after exploring several potential educational/vocational/career pathways and associated feasibility and implementation issues, and after ensuring the client has a responsive context and the necessary skills to pursue the goal" (Vondracek & Ford, 2019, p. 441). Clients may need to be provided with information about resources they can access as they work toward setting and achieving their goals. "Students can apply their career-related knowledge by completing project-based learning activities that involve goal-setting and pursuit strategies" (Howard & Dinius, 2019, p. 169).

One of the earliest models of career decision-making was Parsons's (1909) tripartite model which essentially involved knowing about yourself, knowing about the world of work, and making a sound decision based on those two sets of information. This "matching" model has essentially underpinned career decision-making to the present day. Parsons encouraged people to collect and reflect on a vast array of information about themselves, and the need for information gathering in goal setting and decision making has not diminished since that time. To clarify, information gathering involves exploration with clients about their past and present life, work, and learning experiences, with a view to considering their preferred future. Information gathering in contemporary career practice involves encouraging clients to tell holistic, contextually, and culturally grounded stories to support a process that goes beyond matching on the basis of a limited number of variables. An outcome of this exploration process is an enhanced understanding of the client and their needs and possibilities for the future, which can inform goals and potential action steps. It is important to "set meaningful goals. Encourage clients to identify a goal and develop steps for achieving it. Ask them whether they feel confident that they can complete the steps successfully and whether they will commit to taking those steps" (Niles et al., 2019, p. 293).

> *Choose small steps to begin the next chapter.* Setting a goal is only as helpful as the actions that the client takes toward the goal. Help the client to identify two or three small steps, recognize that there may be obstacles, brainstorm resources that can be used to manage these obstacles, and monitor progress. If a step has not been accomplished, maybe it was not the right first step. Restructure the step and try again. (Brott, 2019, p. 82)

Evaluating Progress

Clients seek career services for a reason, and that reason can indicate a desired outcome. Working toward this outcome may involve taking a series of incremental steps, determined or negotiated across sessions. Evaluating progress, monitoring change, and modifying goals where necessary is important in meeting client needs and maintaining a productive working alliance. Evaluation is about measuring the effectiveness of the client–counsellor relationship and the work they are doing together to achieve the goals they have set, with a view to making changes or modifications if necessary. Evaluation is sometimes presented as the final step of counselling; however, "if evaluation occurs only at the end it is too late" (Egan, 2019, p. 59). Evaluation as an ongoing process is integral to career practice.

Evaluation can help us to answer the question "What progress is the client making, or has the client made?" (Miller, 2019, p. 259). Evaluating progress, therefore, is an essential part of the working alliance within and across sessions and provides feedback on practitioner effectiveness, client participation, and progress and outcomes (Egan, 2019). Evaluation can reveal achieved goals, new goals, changed goals, and processes or techniques that do not work for the client. Evaluation can also be used to determine when the client–counsellor relationship can be terminated because the client's goals have been achieved.

Both the client and the career practitioner have a role to play in evaluation, and a stance by both that is open to feedback facilitates effective evaluation and might lead to adjustments in the working alliance or client goals. Catering better to client needs, ensuring progress toward goals, and improving practice can all be outcomes of effective evaluation. By helping clients to notice progress, evaluation strengthens a client's sense of personal agency and encourages them to progress in their career transitions.

> *Monitor implementation.* *Help clients to document their goals and plans and to develop a system to monitor progress regularly.* (Niles et al., 2019, p. 293)

Evaluation can be undertaken in a variety of ways. For example, Miller (2019) suggested the use of scales in her solution-oriented approach. Formative evaluation can help to monitor progress, provide a sense of direction, and identify what is working and what is not working for clients and practitioners. Formative assessment can be undertaken at the end of each session and can be guided by simple questions such as "What have we achieved?"; "How did this session go for you?"; or "What has been helpful and what has not been helpful?" Summative evaluation is usually undertaken at the completion of a career intervention and provides an opportunity to assess progress, celebrate achievements, and chart a course for the future.

Conclusion

There is widespread agreement on the value of quality client–practitioner relationships to ensure the development of effective working alliances and that clients are progressing toward the achievement of their goals; "relationship building is not a single step but is essential to work on throughout the counselling process" (McMahon & Patton, 2019, p. 247). Building client–practitioner relationships is an iterative process which strengthens the relationship over time. Relationship building is a shared responsibility of clients and practitioners. Cultivating effective working relationships is likely to be rewarded with better outcomes for clients.

Career Development Practice Is Built on Relationships:
Reflection Questions

Revisit the personal vignette you created in Chapter 1. Use the following questions to apply the content of this chapter to your vignette.

1. Think of a time when you had an effective practitioner–client relationship. What did you do to facilitate the relationship?
2. How do you understand your role in establishing effective practitioner–client relationships?
3. What steps would you take with a client to build an effective relationship?
4. How would you explain the practitioner–client relationship to a colleague?
5. How would you explain the practitioner–client relationship to a client?
6. How would you explain the working alliance to a colleague?
7. How would you explain to a client their role in the working alliance?

Chapter 4

Career Development Practice Involves Collaboration With Clients

Career development practice involves close collaboration with your clients—walking alongside, or *with*, them rather than doing things *for* or *to* them. The focus of Chapter 4 is to:

- Emphasize the need to identify and explore the unique personal characteristics and contexts of your clients
- Encourage taking a strengths-based approach that focuses on each client's competencies and skills
- Highlight the key role of client motivation in successful career development
- Recognize the impact of a client's readiness for change

As you read, pause periodically to reflect on the personal vignette that you created in Chapter 1. Consider how working collaboratively with your client might be helpful in that scenario or how the content below applies to your own career development. Questions for further reflection are listed at the end of the chapter.

A Focus on Clients

Clients play a key role in psychotherapeutic outcomes (Fuertes, 2022); the same could be argued in career counselling and coaching, where a collaborative relationship between clients and those who are helping them is crucial. Each client is unique; to be effective in our work with them, as described in Chapter 3, building a strong working alliance is an essential first step (Milot-Lapointe et al., 2020). With that working alliance in place, you can begin to collaborate with your clients to explore their personal characteristics and contexts (Bakshi & Fialho, 2019) and to surface the preferred futures that they are hoping to create. Asrowi et al. (2021) identified seven career counsellor competencies that contribute to client success: attending, leading, reflecting, summarizing, interpreting, confronting, and informing/advising. When grounded in a solid working alliance, these professional competencies can be leveraged to build a collaborative relationship that brings to light the strengths, challenges, contexts, and concerns impacting your clients' career development. This chapter examines how the personal characteristics of your clients, along with their competencies and transferable skills, motivation, and readiness for change, impact the collaborative work you do together to facilitate their career development.

Personal Characteristics

As noted by Goodman (2019), "The self comprises the qualities of the individual. These may include cultural factors, demographic characteristics, psychological resources, and resilience" (p. 134). Career development professionals acknowledge clients as the experts on themselves (Arthur, 2019b, p. 30). Therefore, it is important to collaborate closely with your clients to identify the contextual factors or personal characteristics they choose to prioritize in planning the next stage of their careers, and to identify strengths, limitations, and guiding values (Goyer & Dumas, 2019).

Both constraints and opportunities will emerge in your collaborative exploration with clients; these may include "gender, social circumstances, cultural identity . . . and [such contextual factors as] historical time and place" (Bakshi & Fialho, 2019, p. 40). Interests are often taken into account in career decision-making. As Chen and Hong (2019) noted, "Interests are a key component in career autonomy. As such, career counselling addresses the existence and impact of interest in career choice, exploration, and decision-making situations, while recognizing other influ-ences that can facilitate or hinder individuals' interest[s]" (p. 92). After working with your client to identify their interests, it can be helpful to use tools such as the National Occupational Classification system from Canada (https://noc.esdc.gc.ca/), or equivalent resources in your country or region, to identify educational programs and occupations that fit with their interests and preferred personal styles (Nauta, 2019).

The client's level of agency – their perception of control over their actions and consequences – is also important in determining "how much effort . . . the client [will] need to exert to access and travel on selected pathways" (Bakshi & Fialho, 2019, p. 40). Through collaboration with your clients, you can take a strengths-based approach (Amundson, 2019), "encouraging [them] to relate to their thoughts, feelings, life situations, strengths, dreams, and goals" (Kattelus. 2019, p. 182). In working with individuals during any type of career transition, it can be helpful to normalize anxiety and "not knowing" (Luken & de Folter, 2019, p. 205), as well as to assess their readiness for change (a topic we will return to later in this chapter). Grounded in a solid working alliance, you and your clients can collaborate to set goals and strategies that will feel doable, helping your clients to feel more focused and confident about achieving their goals.

The developmental stage of your clients is another important consideration. For example, "the developmental stage of adolescent students and their brains implies that many of them are not yet capable of making well-balanced long-term decisions" (Luken & de Folter, 2019, p. 205). Interventions designed for youth or first-time career entrants would not likely be a good fit for midcareer workers. Likewise, career growth initiatives may not suit older workers who, although not quite ready for retirement, are no longer interested in accumulating overtime hours or aspiring to upward mobility in their careers. McCoy (2019) emphasized a holistic approach to learning more about your clients and their coping resources, paying attention to "the psychological, psychosocial, academic–vocational, and financial levels of development" (p. 236). The focus here is intentionally on developmental stage rather than age; individuals will have different needs depending on their life stages and contexts.

It is also essential to help your clients examine their career plans within the context of relationships and of responsibilities related to significant life roles outside of work, identifying "key life dimensions (health, family/couple, social, financial, spiritual, personal growth) to focus on" (Goyer & Dumas, 2019, p. 145). Bakshi and Fialho (2019), for example, invite the consideration of linked lives: "How are the pathways that the client chooses connected to, impacted by, or impacting the pathways others in his/her life have chosen or wish to choose?" (p. 40).

> **Relatedness occurs in context.** *Help clients to notice, and actively include, various relational aspects in the big picture of a career problem and career decision-making process. A career plan is formed and action is taken in conjunction with relational and contextual influences involved in given situations. (Chen & Hong, 2019, p. 92)*

Competencies and Transferable Skills

Each individual with whom you work will have a unique combination of competencies and skills. Sometimes, however, working independently clients will find it impossible to identify their own strengths or gaps. By working collaboratively with a career development professional, clients can come to know their skills, recognize how they apply within the current labour market, and describe them in a way that clearly articulates to potential employers the value they add to the workplace.

> ***Enhance career competency.*** *Help clients gain, further, and polish concrete skills in building and managing their life-careers. The career counselling process reinforces and facilitates clients to become intentional, transformative, and lifelong learners who are better equipped with pertinent skills to encounter issues, changes, and challenges in the real world of work."* (Chen & Hong, 2019, p. 92)

Many career development theories incorporate processes for identifying and strengthening a client's skills and competencies. Maree (2019), for example, employed a narrative approach to "elicit clients' (auto)biographies . . . to help them uncover undeveloped or 'hidden' capacities" (p. 226). Miller (2019), on the other hand, employed structured questions to engage clients in recognizing past successes and, specifically, what they had done to result in those successes (p. 259). In an organizational setting, Bernes (2019) recommended creating "a database of employee competencies" (p. 51); a similar approach could be helpful as you work with your clients to organize their skills and competencies in such a way that they can easily retrieve them when writing targeted resumés or preparing for job interviews.

It is often said that our clients are the experts on themselves and on the occupations that they choose, and that career development professionals contribute expertise about the labour market as well as the career development and job search processes. This partnership can be critical in identifying the specific skills and competencies that employers are seeking — and then articulating those competencies in language that the employer will recognize and understand (Woodend, 2019). Many skills and competencies are transferable across sectors and specific jobs; many countries have developed frameworks that offer common language for describing skills that employers tend to value such as adaptability, problem-solving, collaboration, communication, and digital literacy (see Canada's Skills for Success as one example; Government of Canada, n.d.b). Watson and McMahon (2017) used a structured interview process to support clients to reflect on their career transition stories, with a particular focus on adaptability and resilience. Career development practitioners can also assist clients to compare job descriptions with the skills and competencies that they've acquired through previous work and other life experiences to then target resumés, cover letters, and interview responses in ways that clearly demonstrate a relevant match.

> **Consider ways in which you could creatively re-combine your/your client's current knowledge, skills and abilities,** *that may lead to a new narrative and possibilities in the labour market. By changing one's perspective on one's experience and skill set, hitherto unappreciated transferable skills can be revealed. This can open up new and unexpected opportunities.* (Pryor & Bright, 2019a, p. 357)

Despite working from a strengths-based perspective, career practitioners and their clients may recognize gaps between the client's current skill levels and those needed to successfully achieve career goals. Goyer and Dumas (2019) recommended being specific about both the generic and technical skills to be developed and then articulating plans to acquire and master those skills. Similarly, Woodend (2019) highlighted the importance to a person's *lifelong* career development of upgrading skills "to bring their abilities in line with work-environment requirements [as] work environments are always changing and people's skills need to stay in sync" (p. 462).

Not all learning requires formal education. Career practitioners can help clients to recognize and access different types of learning experiences. Clients can be encouraged to learn through observation, hands-on practice, listening to others, and even through self-reflection about their feelings and physiological reactions to specific situations; through a mix of learning opportunities designed to enhance their self-efficacy, they can begin to trust in the possibility of positive outcomes (Sheu & Wang, 2019).

In addition to specific work-related skills and competencies, it can also be helpful to teach clients career development skills that will help them self-manage their careers in the future, long after their work with you has been completed. For example, cognitive information processing (CIP) practitioners "share elements of the approach to empower their clients with skills that can be applied to future career decisions" (Osborn, Dozier, Bullock Yowell et al., 2019, p. 306). Magnusson and Redekopp (2019) recommended that practitioners directly teach clients how to clearly speak about their own skills, recognize opportunities, creatively bridge their assets and the available opportunities, document the effectiveness of those bridges, and communicate their successes to others. As Osborn and her colleagues (2019) highlighted, "Skills can be learned. Effective career decision-making and problem-solving are teachable" (p. 306).

Motivation

Lifelong career development can be hard work; it can take effort to continuously review and assess one's career and reposition it when necessary. As implied by the word lifelong, that work is never done, and part of your role as a career development practitioner may be teaching your clients a career development process to continue moving toward their preferred future and career-life goals (Howard & Dinius, 2019, p. 169). To foster motivation, assessment may include a focus on meaning and purpose (Maree, 2019) and an exploration of "your client's personal interests, passions, and desires" (van Brussel, 2019, p. 422). Attending to emotions in career counselling — offering space to express them and collaboratively working to manage them — is also important (Olry-Louis, 2018). Similarly, Domene and Young (2019) noted that "emotion energizes, which makes it important for career counsellors to work directly with clients' emotions and emotional memories" (p. 124).

Providing a safe space for emotions, positive or negative, to surface can help clients to process them, learn from them, and manage them more effectively should they arise in job interviews, at work, or in other life roles. As noted by Luken and de Folter (2019) in their discussion of acceptance and commitment therapy (ACT) as applied to career counselling, "It's more about better feeling than feeling better. Thinking often mitigates or even distorts feeling. Focus on direct experience rather than abstract understanding" (p. 205). Supporting your clients to integrate their thoughts, feelings, and behaviours can help them to stay motivated throughout their career changes and transitions.

Sometimes individuals may appear to have lost their motivation to move ahead with their career plans because they are caught in a "relational paradox. Career dilemmas may arise due to the desire to remain in connection with important others (e.g., parents, partner), while at the same time avoiding decisions that they might disapprove of" (Popadiuk, 2019, p. 336). Working collaboratively with your clients to identify conflicting priorities and other concerns can help to generate new perspectives and possibilities, freeing clients to find a new pathway forward. When working directly with individual clients, always keep their contexts in mind, including the career impacts of their many relationships and non-work-related life roles. The importance of reflecting on your practice was highlighted in Chapter 2; Chapters 7 and 8 will further examine the significance of culture and context.

In examining motivation, consider the role of agency: "How much effort will the client need to exert to access and travel on selected pathways [and] is the client drawn to newer or well-trodden pathways, and why?" (Bakshi & Fialho, 2019, p. 40). In an in-depth analysis of a single case in life-design counselling, do Céu Taveira et al. (2017) identified that a key to effective collaboration was recognizing and working within the client's "therapeutic proximal development zone" (p. 1); Vygotsky (1978) described the zone of proximal development as the space where an individual, with support or scaffolding to make the learning neither too challenging nor boring, had the capacity and motivation to learn. Therefore, it is important to work with your clients to "plan manageable adjustments, aim[ing] for some 'quick wins' to strengthen motivation" (Neault & Pickerell, 2019, p. 281). This can sometimes surface values conflicts between you and your clients; keep engaging in self-reflection about your own assumptions, priorities, and career-related beliefs so that you do not find yourself imposing (or projecting) your personal values onto your clients but, rather, can discern how to use your values effectively to support your clients' success. Chan and Hedden (2023) identified that successful career advisors were able to navigate values conflicts through "masking, moderating, or magnifying their values" (p. 276) according to the unique needs of their clients. This fits with the concepts of both agency and scaffolding as well as with your client's readiness for change, which will be discussed in the next section. You and your clients may have very different perceptions about agency or about capacity and readiness for change. Discerning whether to mask or moderate your personal values, or to share them with your clients as a source of encouragement and role-modelling, is essential in taking a client-centred approach.

Even the most motivated individuals may find their motivation waning at times; career changes are challenging and rarely go completely according to plan. As career professionals, watch for shifts in motivation, offering both regularity (to build habits and consistent progress) and variety (to enhance interest and reignite energy; Luken & de Folter, 2019), as well as "positive feedback, making the client's goals explicit, and affirming the client's competence" (Vondracek & Ford, 2019, p. 441). Also consider the role of rewards and incentives in keeping your clients motivated, recognizing that these will be unique to each individual — and may differ across their life stages and circumstances; something that previously served as a motivator may not do so in a client's current contexts.

Hammond (2014) applied the stages of change model developed by Prochaska and DiClemente, (1982) to career development work, finding it especially helpful for clients who are feeling stuck and demotivated, struggling to move through the career change process. Six stages of change for individuals are identified in the model: (a) Precontemplation – being unaware of the need for change; (b) Contemplation – recognizing a problem; (c) Preparation – beginning to make a decision

> *Rewards count. Explore the wide scope of rewards that bring people to, and keep them in, work environments (i.e., beyond financial; include personality styles). What people find rewarding is often related to their values and the meaning of work for them in the contexts of their current lives.* (Woodend, 2019, p. 462)

about next steps; (d) Action – engaging in behaviours that will lead to change; (e) Maintenance – working through issues until the problem has been resolved; and (f) Termination – when the individual no longer needs support with that specific change. A reluctance to engage in interventions or activities related to a career change could indicate a challenge with readiness to change.

Motivational interviewing (MI) is an approach that facilitates collaborative, goal-oriented communication with individuals who may be ambivalent about a change. MI is often used to help individuals move through the six stages of change. In a study of individuals who were unemployed and considered not yet ready to seek employment, Britt et al. (2018) found that MI "increased motivation for employment, employment program participation, and employment and employment retention" (p. 176). In a study of career practitioners with MI training, more change talk was noted in clients, suggesting that this may be a useful area of further skill development for career development professionals hoping to enhance their clients' motivation and readiness for change (Britt et al., 2023).

Readiness for Change

> **Career counselling is all about life changes.** Any career development intervention aims, above all, to help people make conscious and meaningful changes in their personal and professional lives. (Cournoyer & Lachance, 2019, p. 101)

Clients often access career support when they are in the midst of significant career or life transitions and, as discussed above, at various stages of readiness. In Goodman's (2019) discussion of Schlossberg's 4S model, "transitions are universal and a common part of life. Everyone experiences transitions throughout life, some big and some small. They are common to all, yet unique to each individual" (p. 134). It is important, therefore, to consider your client's change readiness (Osborn, Dozier, Bullock Yowell et al., 2019) and to surface strategies that may have worked in similar situations in the past (Goodman, 2019). Working collaboratively, you can optimize transitions by "capitalizing on potential turning points" (Bakshi & Fialho, 2019, p. 40) and avoid repeating unproductive patterns from the past. Some transitions will be more gradual than others; Riverin-Simard and Simard (2019), for example, encouraged paying attention to even small shifts in perception about one's work or workplace, recognizing that such shifts could trigger future career changes "even if [clients] are currently in no way ready to undertake such a change" (p. 377).

"Transitions are normative and non-normative" (McCoy, 2019, p. 236); the non-normative ones can be particularly challenging for your clients as they have access to fewer role models. Some transitions, as described in Schlossberg's 4S model, may be nonevents (Goodman, 2019); for example, not being accepted into a desired university or program, an anticipated promotion that doesn't come through, or the loss of a spouse thwarting upcoming retirement plans. In cases of non-normative or nonevent transitions, your client will likely be grieving a loss — and may be quite alone in that grief if the anticipated or preferred future had not been shared with many others. Until your client has had time to work through the loss, and the accompanying grief, trying to set goals or implement career plans may be near impossible. As previously addressed, it is important to accept clients where they are, acknowledging that they may differ in terms of their readiness for change.

Accessing and amplifying a client's hope is a vital change-readiness step; hope is one of the most significant predictors of successfully navigating change (Magnusson & Redekopp, 2019). It can be particularly helpful to have your client "envision future possibilities [and] doing the best job they could possibly imagine" (Niles et al., 2019, p. 293), reflecting on the specific factors that make that job so appealing. Alongside hope, confidence or a sense of agency helps people to take action; providing descriptive feedback of the strengths you see in your client, as previously discussed, can go a long way in bolstering confidence (Magnusson & Redekopp, 2019).

Sometimes your clients will not yet be ready for a major career change nor even for taking a significant next step along their career development journey. In a study that investigated counsellor–client agreement on work capacity in a sample of individuals living with serious mental health challenges, Millner et al. (2020) found only moderate agreement, highlighting that the client and the helping professional may evaluate readiness quite differently. It is important, therefore, that assessment of your client's readiness for change be a collaborative effort. Although you will likely see strengths that your client has not yet identified, your client may offer important insights about day-to-day challenges that would not be apparent during the brief opportunities that you have to meet and personally observe their readiness and capacity for work. At the same time, you might have important insights to offer about potential barriers to employment that your client may be unaware of (or not ready to acknowledge). Conversations about such disconnects can be very challenging. For example, some career practitioners find it particularly uncomfortable to discuss personal presentation or career image with clients but will proceed with such discussions if they believe it will contribute to their clients' success (Yates & Hooley, 2018). Once again, this highlights the importance of a strong working alliance as the foundation for your collaborative partnership (see Chapter 3 for more information on this); without it, you may tend to either avoid uncomfortable conversations or present information in a way that your client will be unable to hear or act upon.

Conclusion

Working collaboratively with clients is emphasized in a wide range of career development theories and models. Clients bring expertise about their own lives and contexts; career development professionals contribute expertise about career development processes and labour market realities. Grounded in a solid working alliance, and working from a strengths-based perspective, you can create a safe and effective space to examine your clients' personal characteristics, contexts, and career considerations; explore and, when necessary, enhance their motivation; and assess and accommodate their readiness for change.

Career Development Practice Involves Collaboration With Clients: Reflection Questions

Revisit the personal vignette you created in Chapter 1. Use the following questions to apply the content of this chapter to your vignette.

1. How has attending to the unique personal characteristics and contexts of your clients helped you to foster collaborative relationships with them?
2. What strategies have you found most effective in facilitating a strengths-based approach?
3. Reflect on a time when a client seemed particularly motivated to collaborate with you in working towards a career goal. What fuelled that motivation?
4. Reflect on a time when a client seemed particularly unmotivated or seemed to lose motivation. What contributed to that? Were you able to work together to turn it around? If yes, how? If not, what were the challenges?
5. Identify three to five factors that may be impacting a client's readiness for change. What types of support/scaffolding might help your client to engage in a change process?

Chapter 5

Career Development Practice Requires Customization

Career development practice is not "one size fits all." Rather, effective approaches and interventions are customized to meet the unique needs of clients within their current contexts. The focus of Chapter 5 is to:

- Situate career development practice within an era of customization and accommodation
- Highlight the benefits of customization
- Emphasize the importance of collaborating with our clients to customize programs and services
- Examine the process of customization, acknowledging pragmatic considerations and constraints

As you read, pause periodically to reflect on the personal vignette that you created in Chapter 1. Consider how taking a customized approach to career practice might be helpful in the scenario you chose to examine, as well as some of the constraints impacting your ability to customize. Questions for further reflection are listed at the end of the chapter.

An Era of Customization and Accommodation

In many parts of the world today, individuals have become accustomed to having several options to choose from in all life contexts — from the sandwich toppings at a fast-food restaurant to the features to incorporate into a custom-built home. Even dating apps quickly and efficiently cater to individual choices and preferences. Many professional service providers (e.g., counsellors, physiotherapists, physicians) use online booking applications that enable clients/patients to choose appointment times that fit with their schedules, and some universities even grant students a great deal of flexibility in building their course schedules and, in some cases, degrees. Online shopping options can deliver a wide selection of international products right to your home via your phone or personal computer.

Concurrent with this abundance of daily opportunities to customize products and services are concerns about inequities in people's access to education and employment. Such inequities have highlighted the need to overcome social and structural barriers through accommodations for individuals and communities who are disadvantaged, marginalized, or otherwise vulnerable in society. It is likely not surprising, therefore, that public employment-service-providers have followed suit — especially in developed countries where choice has become a prioritized value. For example, in a small qualitative study with youth in foster care, Williams et al. (2018) reported that their participants found customized interventions quite valuable. Toh and Sampson (2021) noted, however, that "while public employment service delivery in many developed countries today is rendered in a differentiated, needs- or profile-based approach, it remains entrenched in a traditional one-size-fits-all, first-come-first-served approach in most developing countries" (p. 90). It could easily be argued that customization is not as prevalent in many developed countries as these authors suggested. Globally, the career development sector has room to grow in customizing practices and processes to better meet the needs of the diverse range of clients we serve. One promising example of a client-centred, needs-based, and customized approach to preemployment programming is In Motion and Momentum+, developed by the Canadian Career Development Foundation (Palmer & Klinga, 2022). Although it is cohort-based and follows a standard curriculum outline and schedule, there is much room within the program for participants to shape their own learning experiences and career interventions.

Whether you work in developed or developing contexts, you can efficiently and effectively meet the needs of your clients by customizing your practices, taking a client-centred approach in all that you do, and always taking into account process and context considerations.

Customization Practices

Customization comes in a variety of "sizes," beginning with such basic adjustments as using plain language to facilitate your clients' learning and understanding about career development processes and possibilities. Customized experiential learning opportunities can engage your clients in memorable activities. Finally, you can continuously add to your own toolkits and resources to have more options available to meet the needs of the individuals you serve. All of these ideas will be expanded upon below.

Adjust Language
Find creative ways to match your clients' use of language, without being patronizing or insensitive. Poehnell (2019) highlighted the importance of using "language that is accessible to those you work with. Avoid technical language (such as skill or assessment) that people may not understand. Watch for trigger words (such as education) that may raise defensive barriers" (p. 326).

Strive to use *plain language.* The Government of Canada (n.d.a), for example, dictates the use of plain language in all public communications and the International Plain Language Federation (n.d.) "promote[s] the public benefits of plain language and improve[s] professional practice." It is important to attend to words, structure, and also graphic design elements when communicating in plain language; the primary question to ask yourself is, "Will the person receiving this be easily able to find and use the information I am sharing?" The key to customizing reading level is to use age-appropriate language and design. When writing for an adult audience but at a Grade 8 reading level, you would still use adult words, design, and examples — you are not writing for children but rather adjusting the level of reading difficulty to accommodate adults who may have lower literacy or be learning your local language.

In adjusting language levels, it is also important to distinguish between the needs of adults with lower literacy and those who are very well-educated but communicating in a language other than their primary one. The accommodations these two groups need are quite different, although a plain language approach that simplifies sentence structure and avoids ambiguous words, jargon, or overly tech-

> **Negotiate common language.** *Notice the language that your clients use. There are multiple meanings of career, jobs, work roles, and occupational success.* (Arthur, 2019b, p. 30)

nical language can be helpful for both. Adults with high literacy in another language may be quite comfortable using translation tools and dictionaries, and finding information online or in books. They may also read at a higher level than they speak. Adults with low literacy, on the other hand, may have a limited educational background or be struggling with a learning disability, perhaps undiagnosed. They may have learned to hide their reading difficulties, perhaps not acknowledging them to you. If they are not reading what you've asked them to, have not completed forms or written activities, or seem to ignore your written instructions, it can be natural to interpret this as lack of motivation or even non-compliance/resistance. Instead, consider the possibility of reading difficulties, adjusting language where you can, or referring them to literacy supports.

Matching your clients' language and style may also include using metaphors. Both Amundson (2019) and Spangar (2019) encouraged the practice of communicating with clients through metaphors, incorporating and building on their own metaphors wherever possible.

> **Use metaphors creatively.** *Are you paying attention to the metaphors you hear from your clients and also being more intentional with the metaphors that you use? Are you able to use metaphors to summarize stories? Do you know how to use drawings and physical activity to elaborate, extend, and change the metaphors that you are hearing? (Amundson, 2019, p. 9)*

Facilitate Learning and Understanding

Another way to customize your practice is to meet your clients where they are now and collaborate with them to deepen their understanding — of themselves, their contexts, and the career development process. Move away from a "one-size-fits-all" programmatic approach to a customized approach that builds on existing client strengths and fills in specific gaps to bridge your client's path toward achieving their unique goals. This is, in Nauta's (2019) words, a way to "promote optimal career development" (p. 270). You may achieve this by facilitating self-reflection and encouraging mindfulness (Niles et al., 2019), systematically using assessment tools (Dionne & Dupuis, 2019; Healy & McIlveen, 2019), or providing information (van Brussel, 2019). You might also customize lesson plans and learning resources (Kattelus, 2019), or, when appropriate, explain the career development models and theoretical concepts that you are using in ways that will help your clients to make sense of their experiences and take relevant steps toward their goals (Neault & Pickerell, 2019; Vondracek & Ford, 2019).

> **As much as possible facilitate rather than direct.** *Use your knowledge and experience at a higher level than just telling. Guide people to self-discovery through questions or activities and then affirm their discoveries. This is more effective in building people's self-confidence, as they learn to believe in themselves and in what they can do.* (Poehnell, 2019, p. 326)

As Osborn, Dozier, Bullock Yowell, and their colleagues (2019) emphasized, "Knowledge and process are both essential. Cognitive Information Processing (CIP) encompasses domains of knowledge (knowledge of self, knowledge of options, decision-making, thinking about decision-making) and a process of career decision-making (Communication, Analysis, Synthesis, Valuing, Execution)" (p. 306). An important foundation for career decision-making is good information, both about oneself and also about the labour market and specific occupational/industrial sectors that one is preparing to enter. This focus on information dates back to Parsons's (1909) work in the early 20th century and has carried through to contemporary career practice; see Chapter 6 for more on how Parson's influence continues today.

Many models of career decision-making and career development introduce specific tools and processes to facilitate such information gathering — looking both inward and outward. Pryor and Bright (2019b) highlighted the importance of identifying repeating themes and patterns "to assemble a complex pattern of the client" (p. 357). Healy and McIlveen (2019) use career writing to help clients explore influences on their career to identify helpful and unhelpful personal "I" positions.

> **Responding to and summarising the MCC [My Career Chapter] manuscript is key.** *The crucial stages of MCC are steps five and six, in which the client reads the manuscript to, and hears the response of, their "younger self I-position" before writing a final summary. Leaving it undone may allow unhelpful I-positions to remain unchallenged and conflict between I-positions unmediated.* (Healy & McIlveen, 2019, p. 157)

For many clients, however, simply gathering information will be insufficient to enact change. Sometimes it will be necessary to "assess and address dysfunctional career thinking . . . [to] enhance one's ability to effectively navigate a career concern" (Osborn, Dozier, Bullock Yowell et al., 2019, p. 306). "The key is to encourage the client to articulate their uniqueness to be able to make a contribution that is meaningful and matters to them and to others" (Pryor & Bright, 2019a, p. 357). As career development professionals, you can play a key role in helping your clients to use information about themselves and their careers of interest to deepen understanding of themselves and their career journeys.

Engage Clients in Memorable Experiences

To enhance client learning and deepen understanding, use "sticky" intervention strategies (Amundson, 2019, p. 9). Experiential learning, for example, helps to anchor newly acquired knowledge within a meaningful and memorable context. This can be achieved through customized interventions within your one-on-one sessions or group interventions, or in the community or workplace.

Some interventions are memorable because of the interesting materials they use (e.g., card sorts; Kattelus, 2019; Lengelle et al., 2019). Other activities are memorable because they facilitate a practical application of learning (e.g., project-based learning, work-based learning, field trips,

> **Apply memorable intervention strategies.** *Are you employing memorable (sticky) intervention strategies? Do you have the courage to introduce activities that fall outside the traditional career-counselling box?* (Amundson, 2019, p. 9)

shadowing experiences; Howard & Dinius, 2019). Pope (2019) suggested using occupational-role-modelling and networking interventions "to overcome societal stereotyping as a limitation on occupational choice" (p. 346). Such interventions would be memorable due to the meaningful relationships and conversations they promote.

Design thinking may offer a useful framework for your own customization projects. Over the past several decades, design thinking has been applied to enhance innovation and customization across many industries and organizations (Micheli et al., 2019; Verganti et al., 2021). Although there are various approaches, most entail an empathic, client-centred needs analysis that involves clearly defining the problem, challenging assumptions and brainstorming ideas, prototyping potential solutions, and then testing out those solutions. Recently, several researchers have applied design thinking to career development curricula (Lin & Wang, 2022), interventions (Féja et al., 2023; Kijima et al., 2021), and processes (Conyers et al., 2022). Design thinking fits well with a client-centred approach to career development, collaborating with clients to codesign and experiment with interventions and activities. Be courageous and have fun as you adjust your presentation style, customize your resources, and invite guest speakers to work with your clients, creating experiences that will deepen their learning in memorable ways.

Extend Your Toolkit

Many innovative career development resources are available for purchase. For example, workbooks (Healy & McIlveen, 2019), cards (Kattelus, 2019; Lengelle et al., 2019), and a wide range of assessment tools have been produced, aligned to many different theories and models. There are also sophisticated web-based systems that can be licensed for use in educational institutions or other organizations. Such systems generally include an assessment component that gathers information about an individual's interests, preferences, and perhaps geographic location and then compares that information to databases with information about career and/ or educational opportunities.

Aside from resources for purchase, however, as Luken and de Folter (2019) pointed out, you can "create your own career guidance tools" (p. 205); this is particularly important with emergent approaches, where collaboration is encouraged to bring the theory or model to life, resulting in shared practical tools and resources for use by clients and career development professionals.

Another customization strategy is to mix and match interventions to address the unique needs of your clients. For example, McCoy (2019), in presenting a theoretical approach for working with athletes, acknowledged that "the HAC [holistic athletic career] model is conceptual in nature and does not provide recommendations for client/athlete intervention. However, the HAC model can be supplemented with additional athletic career transition models that include intervention recommendations" (p. 236).

Sometimes your tried-and-true approaches simply do not resonate with a particular client or group. Magnusson and Redekopp (2019) suggested that you "have one or two interventions 'at the ready' for each challenge. These could be as simple as open-ended questions.... such as 'Tell me ... when you were really fired up about the future,' ... 'What's changed for you?'" (p. 216). Similarly, Poehnell (2019) suggested customizing your questioning approach to engage clients who might appear defensive or reluctant. Popadiuk (2019) recommended using "relationally-oriented career questions" (p. 336) to systematically explore your client's career in context.

> *Use surprise experiences to avoid defensive barriers.* Find creative ways to help people who are stuck to discover alternatives and possibilities. For example, asking directly if people feel connected to anyone or anything may result in a defensive outpouring of all their disconnections. It is better to ask what are the possible connections that people may have. This provides an objective distance as they generate a list of possibilities. You can then discuss the list and ask which connections people currently have or can access. (Poehnell, 2019, p. 326)

Client-Centred Customization and Accommodation

Your guide to customization and accommodation will always be your client. By listening to your client's story, customizing interventions that respond to your clients' unique needs, and co-designing with clients, you can contribute to meaning-making and greater personal agency and autonomy.

Start With Your Client

Customization does not always need to involve tools or resources. As Miller (2019) emphasized, "start with what the client wants. It is essential that clients choose their own direction for the interview" (p. 259). Magnusson and Redekopp (2019) used very similar words: "Start with what the client gives you. There is no formal starting point for working with the challenges of coherent career practice, so it is best to simply start with where the client is" (p. 216).

> *Collaborate with clients. Work collaboratively with clients, the real "experts" on themselves (co-construction), by helping them recount (construction) and reflect on their career-life stories (deconstruction), and reminding them that perceived areas for growth should be transformed into strengths (reconstruction).* (Maree, 2019, p. 226)

Listen to Your Client's Story

Each client's story will be unique and nuanced. If you pause and truly listen, every story will guide your efforts to meet your clients' specific needs.

> *Listen for clues in client stories and encourage further storytelling. Listening is more important than talking. Preface story-crafting questions with something in the client's stories that you are curious about. This lets the client know you are listening, builds the relationship, and improves the flow of the interview.* (McMahon & Patton, 2019, p. 247)

McMahon and Patton (2019) emphasized the importance of curiosity, calling you to "act as a curious inquirer to encourage clients to tell their stories" (p. 247). They described individuals' lives as "multistoried" (p. 247); as you listen carefully to clients' stories, you will learn more about their different contexts, the systems impacting them, and the important relationships in their lives. Domene and Young (2019) highlighted active listening — "prob[ing] for the actions, projects, and careers that are central to the presenting issue" (p. 124). Brott (2019) focused on the stories' characters — the people who are important to your clients – noting that "named people can provide perspective by helping the client to see the story from different vantage points" (p. 82); consider, therefore, encouraging your clients to ask some of the people that they mention for information interviews, introductions to others, or insights they might have about your client's next career steps.

When using stories to inform your client-centred interventions and accommodations, remember this:

> **It is the client's story.** The client needs to embrace the life that is being lived and take ownership in how the next chapters will be lived. Change is not needed unless the client chooses to change. Maintaining the status quo may be a valuing decision. Processing emotive responses can lead to insight and to finding meaning. (Brott, 2019, p. 82)

Facilitate Meaning-Making

As you carefully listen for stories, probing to add depth, you and your clients may begin to identify some common themes and patterns (McMahon & Patton, 2019).

Such themes and patterns can surface the underlying meanings of experiences that may otherwise appear unrelated.

Chen and Hong (2019) also emphasized the centrality of meaning-making and the key role you can play as you "help clients identify, clarify, construct, deconstruct, and reconstruct meanings in their life-career experiences, initiating meaningful actions for problem-solving and positive change, leading to the more desirable outcomes in their present and future life-career experiences" (p. 92).

> **Facilitate meaning-making.** *Help clients find their purpose in life, understand the meaning that work brings to them, clarify their future roles, and explore what motivates and inspires them to feel happiness and satisfaction. Give clients space to explore, reflect, and discover their neglected true self.* (Tang, 2019, p. 410)

Promote Personal Agency and Autonomy

During the COVID-19 pandemic, many individuals quit their jobs. In the United States, according to the Bureau of Labour Statistics (as cited in Spinelli, 2022), 48 million people quit their jobs in 2021 alone, resulting in the era being referred to as the Great Resignation. However, from the perspective of agency and autonomy in career development, this period could also be considered a time of Great Inspiration (Spinelli, 2022). As career development professionals, you can support your clients to make proactive career or life decisions rather than simply reacting to environmental influences or trends.

Customization also helps you to "enhance career autonomy" (Chen & Hong, 2019, p. 92) in your clients as you structure interventions that help them to discover who they are and what they can contribute across a variety of career-life scenarios. The concepts of autonomy and agency are interrelated. As Nauta (2019) highlighted, "you can foster agency by helping clients to identify steps they can take to move toward a preferred future" (p. 270). Sheu and Wang (2019) also encouraged "promot[ing] personal agency in career development" (p. 389). Finding creative ways to strengthen your clients' self-efficacy and expectations of positive outcomes can help them "to decide which careers to enter, persist in the face of obstacles, and become satisfied with their careers" (Sheu & Wang, 2019, p. 389).

> **Facilitate agentic actions across life contexts.** *Agentic action is the driver of development. Some actions may not lead anywhere. Other actions may lead to a future life direction in the context in which the action was taken or in another context.* (Richardson, 2019, p. 368).

Agency and autonomy grow from self-awareness and reflection. As career development professionals, you can encourage your clients to try new things out within a reasonably safe environment and then to reflect on their "personal resources and psychological functioning as they interact with their life circumstances" (Cournoyer & Lachance, 2019, p. 101). Facilitating this type of action-awareness cycle can contribute to an understanding within your clients of who they are, who they want to become, and how to navigate that transition with purpose and agency.

Be Responsive

In client-centred customization of career development interventions, the key is to be responsive to your client's unique needs rather than rigidly following a program or being prescriptive about their next steps.

Sometimes you may recognize a pattern of interpersonal challenges in your clients' stories. Consider customizing some activities that will help your clients to "optimize person-environment interaction[s] . . . so that they can build a healthy relationship with others in each layer of their ecosystem" (Tang, 2019, p. 410).

> *Be prepared to respond "in the moment." Because careers are life stories, they are idiosyncratic. Interventions created "in the moment" are often more likely to better address a client's unique needs and context.* (Magnusson & Redekopp, 2019, p. 216)

Many clients feel obligated to follow through on their stated or written plans and goals, worried that others will perceive them as failures if they don't achieve exactly what they set out to do. In a customized, client-centred approach you can "encourage adaptability" (Niles et al., 2019, p. 293), modelling and promoting openness and flexibility in adjusting goals and plans to keep them aligned with a client's top priorities. Being responsive to your clients' stories and customizing relevant activities and experiences can also help them to "break free of restrictions and shift their perspectives ... creat[ing] new mindscapes that reflect their true career interests" (Kattelus, 2019, p. 182).

Client-centred customization can also be helpful at the end of your sessions together or in prioritizing action items resulting from an assessment process. Miller (2019) suggested closing the session by asking, "What now?" (p. 259), and then considering together what it would be most useful to reflect on or to do as a next step.

Process Considerations in Customization and Accommodation

Career Development Is a Process

Although career development professionals recognize that career development is a lifelong process, many clients are seeking instant solutions and might prefer a "one and done" interaction with you. Help them to understand the process of making a career decision and then acting on that decision to get the necessary training and experience to find work and continue to grow in their selected field (Howard & Dinius, 2019). As Lengelle and colleagues (2019) highlighted, "career agency is continually emerging and not a skill to be acquired" (p. 193).

Several theories and models take a constructivist perspective. The underlying philosophy is that there is no single reality or way of living life or pursuing a career; rather, people construct their understandings, purpose, and goals through social interactions. "All theories... [are] about how problems develop and how they can be resolved...Taking action and resolving problems are complementary processes that enhance one another" (Richardson, 2019, p. 368).

> *It's always about going from a first (non-workable) to a second (workable) story and you get there in stages, not in a straight line.* Any time we are learning to tell a new story about our lives and what we are capable of, we are in a nonlinear learning process that takes time, involves emotions, and usually surprises us. (Lengelle et al., 2019, p. 193)

Sometimes, it may be useful to help your clients conceptualize the career development process through illustrations and graphic design elements on posters, handouts, or slides. Many theories and models have accompanying graphics; a few examples include the hope-action model (Niles et al., 2019, p. 284); the career engagement model (Neault & Pickerell, 2019, p. 272); My Career GPS (Goyer & Dumas, 2019, p. 137); the SPARKS chart (Kattelus, 2019, p. 173); the client version of the cognitive information processing (CIP) pyramid of information processing domains and, also, the CASVE cycle (Osborn, Dozier, Bullock Yowell et al., 2019, pp. 296–297); and the systems theory framework (McMahon & Patton, 2019, p. 239).

Many career assessment tools are linked to process considerations. For example, "a thorough assessment of SCCT [social cognitive career theory] variables (e.g., self-efficacy, outcome expectations) will improve clients' knowledge about themselves and their environments, and facilitate their participation in the counselling process" (Sheu & Wang, 2019, p. 389). As Riverin-Simard and Simard (2019) pointed out, a key function of career counsellors is to help their clients recognize the interconnectedness of the various systems they need to operate within, navigate the novelty of the unique circumstances they encounter, tolerate ambiguity, and acknowledge their reactions to unexpected changes — all in all, "the continuous nature of the career transition process" (p. 377). Watson (2019a) invited us to "consider a recycling career counselling process" (p. 452), reminding us of Donald Super's description of minicycles of transition, revisiting earlier stages as our clients navigate the lifelong process of career development.

It Takes a Village

Throughout this book, you'll see a focus on the interconnected systems that impact an individual's career development—careers are neither built nor sustained in isolation. The adage that "it takes a village" can certainly be applied to career development, which makes networking, informational interviewing, and connecting with career influencers very important for both career development professionals and their clients. To successfully activate a village of support systems, it will be essential to "establish communication networks" (Bernes, 2019, p. 51).

Career development begins in childhood and continues even into one's retirement years. As Aravind and Arulmani (2019) emphasized, "Parents count. Help parents to become an acculturative force—to understand how their children's personal strengths and limitations best fit with the world of work, and thereby bring a consonant equilibrium into the lives of their children" (p. 19). Kattelus (2019) also highlighted the impact of engaging family and peers: "Encourage counsellees to share the work that they have completed during counselling, to gain input and new perspectives that might spark new ideas and perspectives about their career options" (p. 182). For example, Kattelus's SPARKS model equips individuals with tangible tools and homework assignments that invite family and friends into the process of career planning, to offer their insights and new perspectives.

> *Connect to daily life. Career counselling is only effective if in-session work is connected to the client's daily life. Counsellors should explicitly focus on this task throughout their work.* (Domene & Young, 2019, p. 124)

To illustrate the value of a supportive network for people with disabilities in particular, consider these examples. In research involving students with disabilities, Khalijian et al. (2023) found that online career counselling mitigated access challenges and had a significant effect on such factors as mental health, employability, and academic buoyancy. Inge et al. (2023), in a study in the United States about the essential elements of customized employment services for persons with disabilities, found agreement amongst service providers about what they perceived to be critical activities but a gap in terms of how consistently those activities are implemented. This suggests that many service providers are not yet adequately trained to provide quality service to people with specialized needs. This is important to acknowledge, for effectively serving all clients, when you are engaged in "creating continuity of services . . . The broadening of the network of contacts and the opportunities offered to the participants contribute[s] to the development and recognition of their skills and help[s] facilitate their participation in training or work" (Dionne & Dupuis, 2019, p. 113). It really does take a village!

Career Development in the Workplace

Lifelong career development is not just about making career plans and securing employment. As career development continues, employers can get involved. Bernes (2019) offered many suggestions for employers. At the strategic level, he encouraged that they "develop and implement an ongoing organizational career development program" (p. 51). At the practical level, he recommended that employers "involve employees in establishing performance expectations" and "provide employees with necessary training and development options" (p. 51).

However, many of your employed clients may work in organizations with no formal career development programs in place. In such cases, you might encourage your clients to request and actively engage in "developmental interviews" (van Brussel, 2019, p. 422). Lifelong career management, as previously discussed, takes a village. Abdicating responsibilities in the workplace to supervisors and managers, or to organizational systems and programs, is less effective than equipping your clients to actively manage and develop their own career pathways.

> **Prepare for an interview.** Encourage your client to prepare for and initiate an interview with his or her manager, and to negotiate personal intrapreneurship and the conditions for its development, in particular the space conditions. The necessary sufficient space for the project should be formulated as a goal or objective. (van Brussel, 2019, p. 422)

Even organizations that are committed to career development struggle to balance employees' needs, organizational needs, and perceptions about employees' performance levels. Straub et al. (2020) examined the impact of customized career services within a professional services firm; this customized approach was designed to facilitate employees' individual career decision-making about whether to increase or decrease pace, workload, location/schedule, and responsibility, with an eye to sustainability. They identified some gender differences in terms of positive outcomes (e.g., fathers who decided to decrease along one or more of the dimensions didn't lose career satisfaction; mothers who made similar decisions to decrease received better performance evaluations). However, they also uncovered some negative career consequences (e.g., flexibility is still stigmatized, especially for fathers who choose a less-traditional path and deviate from the norm of upward mobility). Therefore, as discussed throughout this book, it is essential to keep your clients' context in mind when customizing interventions to support their career development within a specific organization, industry, or occupation.

Conclusion

In an era of customization and accommodation, customized approaches to support your clients' career development can enhance efficiency, effectiveness, and engagement in the process. The practice points cited in this chapter highlighted practices such as adjusting your language, working with your clients to deepen their learning and understanding, applying design thinking to engage your clients in memorable learning experiences and career interventions, and also continuously extending your own career development toolkit. The authors cited also emphasized taking a client-centred approach to customization and accommodation that involves listening deeply to clients' stories, helping them to make meaning of their past experiences, promoting personal agency and autonomy, and being responsive to changes in plans and goals. It takes a village to support career development, and helping your clients to actively engage their support networks can offer a wonderful supplement to their collaboration with you.

Career Development Practice Requires Customization:
Reflection Questions

Revisit the personal vignette you created in Chapter 1. Use the following questions to apply the content of this chapter to your vignette.

1. How do the levels of language you use in speaking and writing facilitate your clients' career development?
2. What types of experiential learning activities have you introduced to your clients?
3. What might make your clients' learning more memorable?
4. As you reflect on clients' needs for customization and accommodation, what are you inspired to add to your own career development toolkit?
5. What strategies might you use to promote your clients' personal agency and autonomy?
6. How can you support clients to respond effectively to changes impacting their goals and plans?
7. Consider one client's "village" of supports. Who else might be invited to contribute to this client's career development? How might they offer support?

Chapter 6

Career Development Practice Is Based on Theory

Theory provides an evidence-based foundation for career development practice. The focus of Chapter 6 is to:

- Articulate why and how career development theory matters in practice
- Consider how theory can guide career development practice
- Provide examples of how theory informs career development practice

As you read, pause periodically to reflect on the personal vignette that you created in Chapter 1. Questions for further reflection are listed at the end of each chapter.

Theory Provides a Foundation for Career Development Practice

Do I really need to learn about theory? Does theory matter to practice? These are questions commonly asked by students in career development classes who simply want to find out how to help people with their career issues. As you read in Chapter 1, a knowledge of and ability to apply career theory is a requirement of professional practice. A knowledge of career theory provides practitioners with ways of understanding and responding to the issues and needs of their clients.

Career development, however, is a lifelong, complex, culturally, and contextually located process, as reflected in this definition:

> Career development involves one's whole life, not just occupation. As such, it concerns the whole person. ... More than that, it concerns him or her in the everchanging contexts of his or her life ... the bonds that tie him or her to significant others ... the total structure of one's circumstances. ... Self and circumstances—evolving, changing, unfolding in mutual interaction—constitute the focus and drama of career development. (Wolfe & Kolb, 1980, pp. 1–2)

Consequently, there are many perspectives on career development and how it unfolds in the lives of individuals. These perspectives form the basis of theories. As explained in Chapter 1, theory has an important role in any professional field; theory essentially seeks to explain a phenomenon (Lent, 2017) and has variously been described as a map, a guide, a model, and a hypothesis.

So, what are some of the perspectives from which career development can be considered in contemporary practice? The original perspective for understanding career decision-making was a model proposed by Parsons (1909), who is widely regarded as the founding father of the field of career development. According to Parsons, sound career decision-making was based on having a good self-understanding as well as knowledge about the world of work (i.e., matching individuals to occupations according to personal traits such as interests, personality, and abilities). Parsons' tripartite model stimulated a trait-and-factor approach to career counselling, later called a person–environment fit approach, that was based on assessing personal traits and then matching them to the characteristics of occupations. Holland's (1997) theory of vocational personalities and work environments is an example of a person–environment fit theory that is supported in practice by the self-directed search (Holland, 1985), one of the most widely used career assessment instruments in the world (see Nauta, 2019).

Another perspective through which to view career development is to take a developmental, age-and-stage approach. Donald Super's (1990) lifespan-lifespace theory is a good example of a developmental approach (see Watson, 2019a) and it identified five career developmental stages across the lifespan as well as the tasks that could be anticipated by people in those stages. Super's idea of lifespace was also significant because it drew attention to the contexts in which careers are enacted and their relationship with other life roles (e.g., spouse, parent, community group member).

Some theories, such as cognitive information processing theory (Osborn, Dozier, Peterson et al., 2019) and social cognitive career theory (Lent & Brown, 2021), focus specifically on career decision-making (see Osborn, Dozier, Bullock Yowell et al., 2019, and Sheu & Wang, 2019, respectively for applications of these theories), with social cognitive career theory paying greater attention to the personal, environmental, and experiential factors influencing career choice.

Attending to the contexts and cultures in which career development unfolds has been emphasized in contemporary theories such as career construction theory (Savickas, 2021), the chaos theory of careers (Pryor & Bright, 2019a), psychology of working theory (Blustein & Duffy, 2021), and the systems theory framework of career development (Patton & McMahon, 2021; see Maree, 2019, Pryor & Bright, 2019b, Blustein, Duffy et al., 2019, and McMahon & Patton, 2019, respectively for applications of these theories).

Some contemporary career theories use culture as their specific focus (see Arthur, 2019b, and Arulmani, 2019, for applications of these theories). The book *Career Theories and Models at Work: Ideas for Practice* (Arthur et al., 2019) contains chapters on a wide range of theories and models and examples of how to apply them in practice.

Evidence-Based Practice

Theories provide an *evidence base* for practice. Career practitioners may work in organizations such as schools and businesses, as private practitioners, and in programs that rely on external funders. Stakeholders such as clients, employers, and funders rightly want to know that career practice is founded in evidence; theory is a way of providing evidence, as most theories have been developed from a research base. Indeed, "change can be enhanced via evidence-based practice" (Blustein, Duffy et al., 2019, p. 72). Evidence-based practice may contribute to better quality service, credibility, and accountability and demonstrate the efficacy of the practice.

Theoretical skills and knowledge can guide you in developing and using interventions that have been researched. The evidence base provided by theories is a lens through which you can conceptualize interventions.

> *Show the theoretical and scientific basis of your practices. Research- and theoretically-based practices can enhance credibility with stakeholders.* (Viviers, 2019, p. 431)

Consider a Range of Interventions

Many theories and models can inform career practice. From a contextual action theory perspective, "interventions from a wide range of sources can be used to resolve problems, as long as those interventions fit within a CAT-informed understanding of the client's situation" (Domene & Young, 2019, p. 124). You have a broad range of interventions from within and across theories to choose from, depending on the needs of each client, and "you can introduce career instruments that you have found to be useful in your practice" (Watson, 2019a, p. 452).

> *Consider a range of career interventions. The C-DAC model encourages you to use a wider range of interventions than are described in the model. For instance, if the client is in the exploration stage or has recycled to that stage, you could consider from among the many exploration activities that are suggested in the career literature.* (Watson, 2019a, p. 452)

Even if you primarily adhere to one specific theory such as the theory of work adjustment, it is possible to "coordinate TWA with other theories to address multifaceted career concerns" (Woodend, 2019, p. 462). In practice, you can consider a range of career assessment instruments and not limit yourself to those derived from one theory or model (Watson, 2019a). You may want to reflect on the theories that inform the resources and career assessment instruments that you use.

Career Development Practice Can be Conducted in Different Formats

Just as there are many different types of interventions, there are also different formats in which career practice can occur. Most commonly, career practice occurs in one-on-one formats, such as career counselling, that are dependent largely on verbal communication. However, formats based on groups, peer groups, pairs, and communities can be considered when people share common concerns. For example, "group career counselling has a strong appeal to many racial and ethnic minority clients" (Pope, 2019, p. 346) and can be applied in community projects and interventions. We invite you to regularly consider the best format(s) through which to address the needs of your clients.

Many theories and models, and the tools derived from them, are versatile enough to "be used in individual career counselling or in group counselling or career education workshops. In group settings, there are added opportunities for peer feedback and social support" (Healy & McIlveen, 2019, p. 157). Interaction between group members, sharing and learning together, can enrich interventions, especially when visual and written interventions are incorporated (e.g., Kattelus, 2019).

> *Realizing a collective project.* The project completed by the group met the needs of a community. It helped counter isolation and allowed participants to be seen in terms of their skills. It also fostered learning and empowerment. (Dionne & Dupuis, 2019, p. 113)

> *Career writing involves creative, expressive and reflective writing exercises and happens in a group.* People read and write in the course together. Reading work aloud is often inspiring but always optional. Feedback on another's writing can be prompted with sentences such as "I like the sound of..." and "I'd like to hear more about." Comment on the text produced, not the person. (Lengelle et al., 2019, p. 193)

Adopt a Holistic Perspective to Practice

Career theorists in general, and contemporary career theorists in particular, tell us that careers are constructed in context. Consequently, when we are working with clients, we need to adopt a holistic perspective in exploring their contextual influences, to gather as much relevant information as possible about their concerns — and to ensure that we do not overlook anything important.

> **Employ integrative interventions that are seamless and natural.** *Work-based issues are rarely separated from nonwork issues, social and economic factors, and relationships. Using inclusive psychological practice, which is based on a thoughtful integration of psychological counselling and work-based counselling, may be optimal for clients facing multiple challenges in life.* (Blustein, Duffy et al., 2019, p. 72)

By way of example, mental health has long been overlooked in career practice. It is important to "remember the centrality of work for mental health. Taking care of your work is essential to preserving your mental health and feeling involved in changing the world, others, or yourself, in a way you have reason to value" (Viviers, 2019, p. 431).

In practice then, "personal and career counselling are closely interwoven" (Maree, 2019, p. 226). To gather a breadth of information from clients, we can "employ integrative interventions that are seamless and natural" (Blustein, Duffy et al., 2019, p. 72) and "view the client and the counselling event in a holistic manner. Acknowledge that 'everything affects everything else'" (Spangar, 2019, p. 400). Practice is strengthened if we "interweave personal and career counselling" (Maree, 2019, p. 226). Although clients may seek assistance to focus on career issues, it is important to consider the interplay of their life roles and relationships.

> **Recognize the importance of environment.** *Interventions should help clients recognize the impacts of proximal and distal environmental factors on their career development, as well as secure resources and cope with barriers to the pursuit of their career goals.* (Sheu & Wang, 2019, p. 389)

A goal of taking a holistic perspective to practice is to "broaden conceptualization.... [to] examine each level of the individual's ecosystem as well as the interaction of these factors" (Tang, 2019, p. 410). One way of doing this is to "consider all life roles. Individuals facing increased challenges in roles outside of work may have diminished capacity for work that was previously engaging. Similarly, increased work responsibilities may result in other, nonwork responsibilities becoming unmanageable" (Neault & Pickerell, 2019, p. 281).

Life roles include those in the family, such as partner, parent, and caregiver, and so we need to "pay particular attention to the role of the family.... [and] the special issues of dual-career couples" (Pope, 2019, p. 346) and "understand the concept of a relational paradox. Career dilemmas might arise due to the desire to remain in connection with important others (e.g., parents, partner), while at the same avoiding decisions that they might disapprove of" (Popadiuk, 2019, p. 336). A useful strategy may be to "encourage clients to connect with other people in their lives about their career paths, as they may gain new information about themselves" (Popadiuk, 2019, p. 336) that could assist them in their career decision-making. Clients' cultural contexts may influence their life roles and the views of others in their networks about their careers. The potential influences of people's cultural contexts are explored in Chapter 7.

> **Use life roles.** *The working life role is just one aspect of the client's life. By opening up the story into all life roles, there are opportunities to situate working as part of the life story.* (Brott, 2019, p. 82)

Career theories offer techniques that support a holistic perspective, such as Super's life career rainbow and archway models. Clients could construct "personalized versions of these models" to holistically explore their life themes (Watson, 2019a, p. 452). Similarly, sociodynamic counselling encourages us to use life-space mapping and visualizations (Spangar, 2019). Life-course theory expounds the value of knowing about life trajectories and applying that knowledge in practice; "observe, study, and read about life trajectories, both of trailblazers and those who follow set paths. Draw on relevant examples during counselling; have clients select and discuss life histories they find fascinating" (Bakshi & Fialho, 2019, p. 40). Guided by Holland's (1997) theory, career practitioners can encourage "clients to learn about themselves and work environments" and "to use hobbies or other life roles to satisfy parts of themselves that are unfulfilled through work" (Nauta, 2019, p. 270).

Consider Integrative Practices

Any student of career development will learn that about a myriad of career theories, each with a particular perspective on career development. Although this can sometimes be confusing, all theories and models offer practitioners useful ways of working with clients. Integrative practice can occur within theories and across theories. As you have seen already in this chapter, theory-based practice is holistic and so clients provide us with considerable information by telling us stories about their lives. As practitioners, we need "to listen 'for' clients' career-life stories rather than 'to' these stories" (Maree, 2019, p. 226). Finding ways to organize the information from client stories can be helpful to us and to clients. One way is to "connect the concepts ... of connection, disconnection, and reconnection [that] provide a basic way of organizing your client's career story" (Popadiuk, 2019, p. 336).

Integration across theories and models occurs when strategies, assessment instruments, or interventions from one theory are introduced to complement what is already occurring in practice based in another theory or theories. For example, relational-cultural theory can be integrated in career development practice, and "this combination offers career practitioners and their clients a new, more integrated way of working together" (Popadiuk, 2019, p. 336). To develop an integrative approach to career practice, read widely, take advantage of professional development opportunities, and reflect on your practice. Chapter 9 provides suggestions for ongoing professional learning.

Contextualize Practice from a Systemic Perspective

Career development is complex and, as we learn from theory, subject to a wide array of systemic influences. Consequently, it is important to "acknowledge the impact of context. Individuals may be concurrently overwhelmed and underutilized (e.g., an overabundance of meaningless tasks)" (Neault & Pickerell, 2019, p. 281). It may be useful early in the career intervention to "de-centre the notion of career, to orient the client toward examining the influences of the many systems that they inhabit" (Healy & McIlveen, 2019, p. 157). Given that influences are dynamic and interact, clients may benefit if we look for connections between the challenges they face: "The challenges interact with and impact each other. When clients understand that interaction, they are less likely to be derailed in their quests" (Magnusson & Redekopp, 2019, p. 216).

Time and timing are also important influences to consider. For example: How long has the issue been present? Is it escalating or diminishing across time? And why is the client presenting with this issue now? It is highly pertinent to "ask 'Why now?' Something has brought the client to counselling. Understanding the current context can help with goal setting, action planning, and prioritizing interventions"

> *Systemic influences can be powerful.* Help clients to view their concerns within larger systems influences to avoid internalizing blame and to address barriers. (Arthur, 2019b, p. 30)

(Neault & Pickerell, 2019, p. 281). In this regard, client motivation is yet another consideration. Chapter 4 discusses client motivation in more detail.

By taking a systemic perspective and gathering comprehensive information about clients, we may come to understand clients' "internal and external resources" and realize that "not all problems (or solutions) reside within the individual. Changes in a variety of interconnected systems may help individuals to re-engage" (Neault & Pickerell, 2019, p. 281). This suggests that, subject to a client's permission, it may be helpful for the practitioner to engage with others such as parents, partners, and workplace personnel. Career practitioners may also take on an advocacy role for clients (e.g., in schools, colleges, universities, or workplaces). You will find more information on advocacy in Chapter 8.

Conclusion

Theory provides a firm foundation for career practice. It enables us to engage in evidence-based practice; it can guide the interventions and formats we use; and when integrated with practice, it can provide a range of options for conceptualizing our cases. With an extensive body of theory that dates back more than a century, career development is well positioned to ground practice in that theory.

Career Development Practice Is Based on Theory:
Reflection Questions

Revisit the personal vignette you created in Chapter 1. Use the following questions to apply the content of this chapter to your vignette and to your own career.

1. How could your career (e.g., stages, influences, experiences) be explained by each of the career theories or models most familiar to you?
2. In what ways do the career theories and models you are most familiar with complement or contradict each other when applied to your career?
3. Are there aspects of your career that you feel are not accounted for by these career theories and models? If so, read about another theory or model you are less familiar with and identify ways in which it might apply to your own career.
4. Identify three career theories or models and reflect on how they could guide your work with a specific client.
5. How would you explain the career theory or model that most informs your work to a colleague?
6. How would you explain to a client how you understand their concerns theoretically?

Chapter 7

Career Development Practice Occurs in Cultural Contexts

This chapter considers ways that people's worldviews and cultural contexts influence their career development. The focus of Chapter 7 is to:

- Orient you to using career resources in ways that account for culture and context
- Explore the influence of clients' worldviews and expertise on their lives and careers
- Acknowledge that people's career development may take multiple pathways
- Discuss how to enhance assessment practices across cultural contexts

As you read, pause periodically to reflect on the personal vignette that you created in Chapter 1. Questions for further reflection are listed at the end of this chapter.

Cultural Context Matters

Theories and models of career development were developed during specific eras and within particular country contexts, shaped by the worldviews, expertise, and cultural beliefs of the people whose ideas informed them. Concerns have been raised about how well theories and models, developed in Western contexts for White and middle-class male populations, apply across countries and populations (Watson, 2017, 2019b). You are encouraged to critically examine the concepts and cultural assumptions that underpin career theories and models (Flores, 2009) and reflect on how well they apply across people's life contexts. To illustrate, values such as independence, autonomy, and logical progression may not be emphasized by people whose worldviews honour collectivist and interdependent values for decision making (Arulmani & Kumar, 2023; Williams, 2003). You might also consider how well theories account for diversity in people's life contexts and their career development, including social and structural barriers associated with gender identity, racialization, ethnicity, social class, sexual orientation, religion, and/or ability, and their intersections (Bimrose, 2019a; Pope, 2019). In recent years, theorists have begun to demonstrate the applications of their work across diverse populations and country contexts (Arthur & McMahon, 2019). In Chapter 6, we gave examples of theories that attempt to incorporate culture and context, along with two examples that position cultural context centrally for understanding people's career development (e.g., Arthur, 2019a; Arulmani, 2019).

In Chapter 2, we emphasized the importance of reflecting on the potential influences of your personal worldview on your professional roles and practices. In this chapter, we will discuss clients' worldviews and the contexts of their lives, as well as assessment processes and practice tools that are culturally relevant for your clients. Career assessment and interventions are based on clients' presenting issues, from their point of view, and incorporate contextual influences in their lives. People express themselves through representations of their life contexts, often told as stories or rich examples based on their experiences (McMahon et al., 2020). The ways that individuals are socialized include key messages, expressed through language and emotion, unique to their family and community relationships. Although you might share many similarities with clients who seek career services, there are inevitable differences, obvious or subtle, in the ways that people understand and experience the world around them. We encourage you to select and use theories and models that support you to assess the life contexts of your clients and to inform relevant career interventions.

Clients and Their Worldviews

Worldview is a concept that generally refers to understandings about who we are, other people, and the world around us (Williams, 2003). People's worldviews are expressions of their cultural identities that are constructed through interactions with other people and experiences across their life contexts (Arthur, 2017). As noted in Chapter 2, it is important for you to be aware of your personal worldview and to be open to the multiplicity of experiences and points of views that matter to your clients. To reiterate, we need to understand people within the contexts of their lives.

> *Reflect on your clients' worldviews. Your clients' socialization influences their views of careers and jobs, and their expectations of professionals.* (Arthur, 2019b, p. 30)

Although people from similar groups might share common characteristics and worldviews, group membership is not an infallible source of information. Making assumptions about people can lead to stereotyping. As noted in Chapter 2, ongoing reflection can help you to recognize similarities and differences between your beliefs and the perspectives of your clients.

Become familiar with the main groups who access your services and those who may experience limitations in career services (Borgen, 2021). Acquiring background knowledge can help you to form insights about "the special issues of the specific cultures" (Pope, 2019, p. 346). At the same time, that general knowledge has limitations. "Guard against stereotypes. A little bit of cultural knowledge can be dangerous. Check out your assumptions as individuals may or may not identify with any group" (Arthur, 2019b, p. 30). Notice when clients might be resisting and not following you, as signs that they may not feel understood or heard, or do not agree with the interventions you are using.

> **Check assumptions.** *Be culturally sensitive by defining values broadly and allowing for individual variation in how these values influence individuals' needs.* (Woodend, 2019, p. 462)

Remember, each new client is an individual who holds a unique worldview. In other words, attending to culture and context is important for working with all clients (Arthur, 2018a). You might approach your interactions with clients with two lenses: one lens to hold background knowledge in tentative ways, and the second to help you assess the relevancy of that knowledge for the individual.

People's lives are dynamic; their worldviews are influenced by many interactions with other people throughout their lives. Similarly, people's sense of connection to their cultural identities may fluctuate over time and across their life roles. In some situations, individuals may feel strongly aligned with some aspects of a cultural identity, and at other times, quite distant from them (Arthur, 2017). Individuals who have experienced discrimination or other forms of cultural oppression may intentionally shift away from being defined by some aspects of their cultural identity (Arthur, 2017). Such experiences and the resulting loss of a cultural identity may be intertwined with clients' career concerns. For example, individuals may feel a "dissonant equilibrium, characterized by poor self-esteem and depleted motivation" (Aravind & Arulmani, 2019, p. 19). Career guidance or career counselling might include exploration of cultural identity in a process that "focuses on strengths rather than deficits" (Aravind & Arulmani, 2019, p. 19). Therefore, you are encouraged to "know the process of cultural identity development and use it" (Pope, 2019, p. 346) in your assessment practices. Above all, remember to "acknowledge client expertise. Clients are the experts on their lives and the ways that their cultural identities and contexts may be relevant for their presenting concerns" (Arthur, 2019b, p. 30).

Career practice relationships can offer clients a platform from which to gain deeper understanding of their presenting career issues, their strengths, and the possibilities for designing meaningful career interventions. Yet, professional relationships are developed within a particular context governed by formal and informal rules about working with people in authority and seeking expert opinion. As discussed in Chapter 3, developing a trusting and supportive working alliance with your clients makes it possible to engage them in a collaborative process to determine culturally relevant goals and processes.

"

Clients' perceptions. *How do your clients view you as a career practitioner? Is the relationship between you and your clients equal? How do you form impressions of them? Power imbalances exist within society along the lines of, for example, gender, age, race/ethnicity, and socioeconomic background. Try to address the power imbalances that will exist in your career counselling relationships with clients.* (Bimrose, 2019b, p. 62)

"

Multiple Pathways

Within a supportive and collaborative working alliance, discussions can focus on "exploring constraints and opportunities" (Bakshi & Fialho, 2019, p. 40). Such discussions might include encouragement for clients to share their experiences and perceptions about education and employment. Notably, there is wide variation in the meaning of work in people's lives; for example, it can be a means for survival income or a source of strong connection to personal identities and thriving (Phillips Davis, 2023). You might encourage clients to describe their perceptions about work, the career pathways they have taken or wish they could have taken, and the perceived challenges and opportunities they encountered. Remember, career exploration includes consideration of key relationships and connections, or "consideration of linked lives. How are the pathways that the client chooses connected to, impacted by, or impacting the pathways others in his/her life have chosen or wish to choose?" (Bakshi & Fialho, 2019, p. 40). Career stories, aspirations, and perceived career pathways may represent strong beliefs about preferred options or barriers — beliefs internalized by individuals through their current or past relationships. The exploration of people's cultural identities might reveal the messages individuals heard from family members, peers, or media, and the relevancy of those messages for present and future career choices (Arthur, 2019a). Notice clients' perceptions about what other people expect of them and how such perceptions are linked to opportunities or constraints.

Support clients to "explore previously unrecognized pathways. Career counsellors may identify potential educational or vocational/career pathways that are not apparent to the client" (Vondracek & Ford, 2019, p. 441). It requires effort to "continue to update yourself about educational and career pathways not just locally, but also regionally, nationally, and globally" (Bakshi & Fialho, 2019, p. 40), but it is through your knowledge base and resources that you assist clients to "consider multiple pathways to the same intermediate stage or endpoint; and to assess the pros and cons of particular pathways" (Bakshi & Fialho, 2019, p. 40). Clients' career goals may or may not change, but clients can be supported to expand their knowledge about strategies for expanding pathways to achieve their career goals. Pursuing new options and their related goals "are often associated with positive feelings and positive evaluations from others" (Vondracek & Ford, 2019, p. 441). Taking a collaborative approach can support clients to initiate new activities and encourage new aspects of their career development. Remember, however, that it is the client's choice about which options to pursue within the cultural contexts of their lives. It is important not to impose your agenda on the career goals or pathways preferred by clients.

> *Aim for the emergence of a new equilibrium. Assess whether fitting into enculturated, socially acceptable educational and career pathways are likely to increase a student's experience of dissonance, placing him or her on a failure rather than success trajectory.* (Aravind & Arulmani, 2019, p. 19)

Methods, Tools, and Assessment Practices

In this chapter, we invite you to consider the application of theories and models across cultural contexts. We also want you to consider other resources, methods, tools, and assessment practices, (e.g., inventories, card sorts, family genograms, collage, metaphors). How familiar are you with the origins of the resources that you use? In what ways do these career resources link to the theories and models that you use in practice? Using the points made in the introduction of this chapter, we invite you to examine career resources from a critical perspective to ascertain *how* they were developed, *by whom*, and for use in *which contexts*. In other words, we encourage you to enhance your cultural competence for selecting appropriate methods, tools, and assessment practices (Evans & Sejuit, 2021).

> **Consider cultural context.** *Clients' family and cultural backgrounds should be taken into consideration in selecting and administering assessments, interpreting assessment results, and designing [social cognitive career theory]-based interventions. Counsellors should also be aware of their own assumptions and biases toward different cultural groups.* (Sheu & Wang, 2019, p. 389)

Remember the need to engage in personal reflection, to become more aware of potential biases that may influence your selected approach to providing career services. For example, although you might have favourite tools that you use in your practice, be open to critically examining them. As suggested in Chapter 5, consider adding resources to your repertoire to help you customize your practice.

We emphasize the cultural applications of the career resources you use. For example, in gaining knowledge about the groups and communities that you serve, "be aware of the special issues when using career assessment inventories with individuals from various cultural communities" (Pope, 2019, p. 346). Also, as emphasized in Chapter 6, you can consider clients' ages and levels of development. For example, "it is important to evaluate the cultural relevance of methods and tools used in career guidance when working with students to match their needs and abilities" (Aravind & Arulmani, 2019, p. 19). To reiterate a key point: select resources and tools that are culturally relevant and matched to clients' presenting issues and to their life contexts. However, it is up to clients to decide if they would like to use particular career resources or tools.

> *Use an ecological assessment.* Collect information regarding barriers and resources from each level of a client's ecosystem in order to identify ecologically valid goals and strategies that will have sustainable outcomes. What constitutes barriers and resources depends on each individual's cultural background and meaning-making process. (Tang, 2019, p. 410)

Assessment doesn't always require specific tools. It is also practised through actively listening to clients' stories about their life contexts. Discussions can help clients to clarify their presenting issues, identify any barriers that they are experiencing, and gain new perspectives about themselves and their current resources. Rather than taking a deficit approach which leads to labelling clients and/or their presenting concerns, "focus on strengths. Identify client strengths that matter to them in their cultural contexts. Build on strengths to grow confidence and competence" (Aravind & Arulmani, 2019, p. 19). Also, build in time to pause during the assessment process to check in with your clients and seek their immediate feedback. You might pose questions such as, "Where are you now? What is happening at this point?" (Miller, 2019, p. 259), using immediacy to help clients gain insights and to check that they feel supported about the process of working with you.

Clients' relationships can be leveraged to help them test out new ideas and check their perceptions of expectations held by other people. For example, given the influence of relationships in clients' lives (see Chapter 5), you might invite clients to identify trusted individuals in their network with whom they feel safe enough to share the goals or processes they are working on or considering (Kattelus, 2019). As noted in Chapters 3 and 5, career services are delivered through multiple modalities and interventions can take different formats. Building connections and support are two reasons that group interventions may have strong appeal for clients who have experienced inequities and/or for customizing approaches to engage people in their communities (Dionne & Dupuis, 2019; Pope, 2019). Group interventions can be useful to identify and normalize common experiences; new and contrasting perspectives can be shared to enhance learning and social support.

You might also help clients to frame their experiences in new ways. For example, many clients internalize blame for their situation, when the career barriers that they face are caused by structural or societal barriers (Arthur, 2019a). Naming those barriers is a form of consciousness-raising to "directly address issues of discrimination.... [and] help clients overcome internalized negative stereotypes or internalized oppression" (Pope, 2019, p. 346). Focusing on client strengths and helping clients to create new narratives about their life contexts helps them to build positive resistance and resiliency for addressing perceived career barriers (Arthur, 2019a). Clients' experiences of inequities and career practitioners' approaches to social justice advocacy are the core topics in Chapter 8.

Organizational Contexts

Lastly, we encourage you to include in the assessment process clients' perspectives about the organizations where they have worked or where they are currently employed. The contexts of work, including organizational cultures, strongly shape people's views about their roles, their current capabilities, or the need for new skill development. For example, when organizations change directions, it is often left up to individuals or groups of employees to adapt to those changes.

Sometimes, the nature of clients' presenting issues requires them to seek clarification about the knowledge and skills required to meet performance expectations in their workplaces. To inform assessment and intervention planning with individuals, you might encourage them to "seek information on [themselves] and feedback from [their] professional environment" (Goyer & Dumas, 2019, p. 145). Groups of employees might also benefit from learning about work performance strategies, including ways "to share their visions and to have input into the organization's vision/outcomes" (Bernes, 2019, p. 51). Supporting individuals to identify workplace performance strategies and to practice the steps involved in implementation can help them to feel more empowered in their work roles.

> **Notice change.** Be mindful of the ongoing changes in work-environment requirements and individuals' needs. This information can help individuals navigate discorrespondence as it arises. (Woodend, 2019, p. 462)

We encourage you to learn about a broad range of employment sectors and organizational cultures. Demonstrating knowledge about employment sectors, such as the "structural, organizational, and policy aspects" (McCoy, 2019, p. 236) builds credibility and can be explored with clients to enhance engagement in the working alliance and intervention planning. Organizational contexts and the roles within them are structured with formal and informal rules that contribute to the culture of workplaces. The interactions between people, including hierarchies and expectations for behaviour in the workplace, are also important considerations for assessment. Adding these additional layers to the assessment process is important because career issues are often intertwined with opportunities and constraints embedded in organizational contexts and cultures.

Conclusion

People develop their worldviews, including values, beliefs, and norms for behaviour, within the cultural contexts of their lives. This is a dynamic process that unfolds over time and across situations. New experiences may prompt dissonance or new understanding about the world of work, career pathways, and potential opportunities or barriers. It is critical for career practitioners to be open to the multiplicity of experiences and points of view that matter to their clients. Career practitioners need to hold general background knowledge about the populations they serve while also attending to the unique worldviews and circumstances of the individuals who seek career services. Multiple levels of assessment can incorporate information about key relationships and experiences in the workplace. Career practitioners are encouraged to select resources (career theories and models, methods, tools, and assessment practices) that are meaningful and culturally relevant for clients.

Career Development Practice Occurs in Cultural Contexts:
Reflection Questions

Revisit the personal vignette you created in Chapter 1. Use the following questions to apply the content of this chapter to your vignette. Consider your personal experiences of career development and/or your role as a career practitioner.

1. How do the career theories or models that you use account for the diversity in people's life contexts and career pathways?
2. What approaches could you use to learn about your clients' cultural worldviews, such as individualism and collectivism?
3. How do you incorporate clients' relationships in discussions about their presenting career issues?
4. What does the phrase "clients are the experts on their own lives" mean to you?
5. How would you respond when a client is pursuing a pathway to a career goal that you feel might not be the best choice?
6. Reflect on the workplace cultures at organizations where you have been employed. How might the contexts in which you have personal experience be similar or different to the organizational contexts where your clients work or want to work?

Chapter 8

Career Development Practice Incorporates Social Justice Advocacy

This chapter emphasizes the foundational concepts of social justice and advocacy for career development practice. The focus of Chapter 8 is to:

- Orient you to the multidimensional concept of social justice
- Critique the meaning and value of work in people's lives
- Connect people's career concerns to sociopolitical contexts
- Provide examples of engaging in social justice advocacy

As you read, pause periodically to reflect on the personal vignette that you identified in Chapter 1. Questions for further reflection are listed at the end of this chapter.

From History to Heroes in Contemporary Career Development Practice

The field of career development has a long history of addressing social inequities and advocating to increase people's access to education and employment. This history extends more than a century, with roots in vocational psychology, often crediting Parsons (1909) for advocacy work with youth and immigrants in the Boston area of the United States. However, during the late1800s and early 1900s, pioneers of social justice advocacy, both men and women, in many other countries, such as Australia, Canada, Japan, England, and Scotland, were training personnel to guide and assist people to find employment (McMahon & Arthur, 2019). History and the heroes of the past paved the way for new forms of vocational guidance and community-based services. Their actions at the time are important examples of how social justice advocacy was integrated into service roles. Unfortunately, some of the same social issues, such as unemployment, inequities in access to education, and poverty, have persisted over many decades.

In contemporary society, a lens of social justice helps us to examine sociopolitical ideologies and influences on education and employment systems (Hooley et al., 2019; McWhirter & McWha-Hermann, 2021; Sultana, 2022). For example, there are debates about the purpose of education: is it a means to foster people's development or fill labour market needs? Yet, the concept of social justice is multifaceted; how we conceptualize social justice has implications for how we design and practice approaches to social justice advocacy (Arthur, 2018b, 2019a). We invite you to consider what you mean when you refer to social (in)justice and how you apply that understanding to practice. Here are five ways that social justice has been represented in the career development literature (Arthur et al., 2009):

- Fair and equitable distribution of resources and opportunities
- Direct action to address oppression and marginalization within society
- Inclusion and participation of all members of society
- Fostering human development and potential
- Engaging people as coparticipants in determining their issues and solutions

Social justice underpins career development practices to address the realities of people's lives and to address social and systemic change (Arthur, 2019a). As career practitioners, you will inevitably interact with people whose lives are influenced by social injustices. When you are working directly with clients, on their behalf, or through educational and employment interventions with the public, your role is intertwined with social justice issues. "The field of career development privileges the idea of social justice as it helps people construct their work lives through the practices of vocational guidance, career education, and career counseling" (Savickas, 2013, pp. 2-3). Career practitioners use their professional knowledge and skills to provide remedial interventions and to help clients adapt and adjust, but also to address the social systems and structures that contribute to people's career concerns (Arthur, 2019a).

Advocacy means giving voice to, and actively participating in, actions that are designed to address social inequities and to promote social justice. Many professional associations have social justice and advocacy statements as part of their ethical guidelines and standards of practice. For example, notice the interconnections between direct service delivery and the workplaces of career practitioners in the following statement: "Thus, social justice is a foundation for supporting clients and the public and for shaping the organizational structures where members deliver educational and guidance services" (International Association for Educational and Vocational Guidance, 2017, para. 2). You are encouraged to review standards of practice and codes of ethics from your professional associations to explore connections between career practitioner roles and advocacy.

Views of Work and the Value of Employment

The meaning of work and its connections to other aspects of people's lives will vary across time and across contexts. In general, employment demarcates legitimate participation in our society, with attendant material or economic benefits, as well as social status and identity. Views of work are often aligned according to the relative economic benefits (along a hierarchy of skilled and unskilled qualifications) and perceived desirability of jobs within and across labour market sectors.

> **Pay attention to how the contexts of work, especially market [paid] work, may be affecting the mental health of your clients.** *Radical social change is altering the nature of market work, causing changes, such as precariousness, that may affect clients' mental health. Clients need help navigating these altered market work contexts.* (Richardson, 2019, p. 368)

The field of career development has emphasized helping individuals to pursue meaningful careers. The reality for many people is that work serves an instrumental purpose—to provide an income—and may not be a source of personal fulfillment. Yet, employment may have direct or indirect benefits through its interconnections to other life roles, such as providing income for family. In other words, work has multiple meanings that overlap with roles and relationships in people's life contexts. As a general consideration, practitioners support clients to explore the "optimal work situation in the context of one's current life" (Goyer & Dumas, 2019, p. 145)

> **Work-based counselling exists along a continuum of self-determination and survival.** *At times, clients will present with work issues related to survival, and at other times, self-determination; counsellors can focus on these needs simultaneously by helping clients to consider short-term and long-term goals, with actions devoted to survival providing clients with a means of developing skills to enhance self-determination.* (Blustein, Duffy et al., 2019, p. 72)

Work takes on many forms, but paid work is generally prioritized and rewarded with higher economic and social benefits. However, societies could not function without people assuming unpaid roles that contribute to family and community care. "In talking to clients about their work, be sure to encompass care work in personal lives as well as market work. Calling attention to care work can validate this typically unconsidered and/or devalued aspect of clients' life experience" (Richardson, 2019, p. 368). Care work, historically and disproportionately relegated to females, may consume hours of labour daily and weekly. The fact that care work is often unpaid should not devalue relational and caregiving roles, as they may be highly regarded by individuals and communities. However, there are differences between what types of work are paid, what work is compensated at low or high levels, and the gendered nature of paid and unpaid work. Practitioners can "focus on work, broadly conceived …. and embrace the full scope of clients' work lives, including caregiving work as well as work that may not reflect a volitional career plan" (Blustein, Duffy et al., 2019, p. 72).

Employment experiences and views of work may vary between you and your clients, and meanings should not be assumed. As emphasized in Chapter 7, meanings associated with work are strongly influenced by social and cultural values, and the values internalized by individuals. The nature of work affords some people the privilege of higher income levels, higher social status, and greater job security. However, many people experience precarious and insecure work, including unemployment or underemployment. Social disadvantage compromises people's access to education and employment, as well as their opportunities for learning and skill development. In other words, people have differential access to educational and occupational pathways which further compromises their future pathways. Career interventions "can help clients maximize their opportunities so that they can experience a level of fulfillment and meaning that is an integral part of our human rights" (Blustein, Duffy et al., 2019, p. 72). Advocates of the decent work movement (Blustein, Kenny et al., 2019; International Labour Organization, 2019;) emphasize employment creation, rights at work, social protection, social dialogue, and gender equity. You might want to consider how this discussion relates to Goal 8 of the 2030 Agenda for Sustainable Development which is to promote employment, decent work for all, and social protection (United Nations, 2015).

Navigating Sociopolitical Contexts

In emphasizing social justice as a foundational value for career development practice, we invite you to examine sociopolitical and structural systems that influence your clients and your service provision. Working with people within their life contexts includes assessing how sociopolitical factors afford opportunities for some people while constraining others. This means exploring the conditions in our society that lead to social advantages, disadvantages, and inequities. We invite you to critically examine the conditions that contribute to people's career distress and help them to access resources and support to address their career concerns (Arthur, 2018b, 2019a). "Individuals are continuously interacting with their life contexts. Career development interventions must take this into account. Individuals are as much determined by their life contexts as by the actions they take within them" (Cournoyer & Lachance, 2019, p. 102). In essence, we cannot isolate individuals, their presenting concerns, or interventions from their life contexts. Navigating sociopolitical contexts requires you to identify the relevant contextual factors and collaborate with clients to increase their sense of agency.

> *Social inequality.* How familiar are you with the social factors in your society that are most strongly associated with social inequality? Understanding the primary sources of inequality and how these interconnect and compound disadvantage (for example, gender with ethnicity) is a necessary step to developing a practice approach that responds to inequality. For example, examine rates of unemployment and the social characteristics of the most vulnerable in your society. (Bimrose, 2019b, p. 62)

A social justice perspective emphasizes sociopolitical influences beyond the individual and their volition. Unfortunately, there are strong social narratives about acceptable behaviour in our society and it is not uncommon for individuals or groups to be blamed for creating their problems. It is important to "help clients overcome internalized negative stereotypes or internalized oppression (Pope, 2019, p. 346). This process can be incorporated into assessment practices to "assess influences of power, privilege, and/or oppression" (Popadiuk, 2019, p. 336). Exploring the relevancy of broader sociopolitical influences can help clients to gain new understandings about their presenting issues and support discussions about relevant solutions.

For example, practitioners need to "be sensitive to cultural learning and enculturation" (Aravind & Arulmani, 2019, p. 19). An illustration of this point pertains to working with a student who experiences a disability and probing their "prevailing career beliefs relating to disability" (Aravind & Arulmani, 2019, p. 19). Such conversations can be empowering for clients as they gain new insights about their history, life context, and presenting issues, through information sharing and education — an intervention known as consciousness raising. Incorporating social justice narratives directly in conversations with clients may help them to reframe their presenting issues and generate possible solutions. This may also be a starting point for working collaboratively with clients to design relevant interventions.

Consider how you can directly address the barriers and constraints in clients' life contexts or in the settings where career practice occurs (Arthur, 2019a). For example, the student from the previous paragraph might benefit directly or indirectly from improvements in the school environment. To illustrate, consider exactly what might be impinging on the student's academic success and limiting their views of occupational choices. You could do this by probing the student's views and providing new sources of information. Also, consider the school setting:

> (T)ry to estimate what some potential academic and vocational achievements could be if some of the barriers in the student's environment (e.g., access to resources, changes to administrative rules) were removed. In this regard, re-evaluate the nature of the current school environment for all students. (Picard et al., 2019, p. 316)

> *Evaluate the capability of finding one's path.* Consider the real freedoms that students have when they choose a path by paying attention to the range of possibilities considered, discarded, or obscured at the time [when] an educational or vocational choice is made, and to the alignment of this choice with their aspirations. Determine if students impacted by some form of inequality benefit from the same or fewer freedoms than their peers. (Picard et al., 2019, p. 316)

To summarize, you will often be working with clients to address their immediate concerns. However, it is important to consider the conditions in people's life contexts and the links between clients' presenting issues and larger sociopolitical issues. Interventions can incorporate empowerment through examining relevant contextual influences and collaborating with clients to reflect on any new perspectives. Also consider how you can actively address the constraints faced by the populations you serve. Some groups, due to how they are positioned in society, do not have the same access to social resources and opportunities to pursue education or employment mobility. It is important to look beyond individual clients to learn more about sources of inequity and solutions that would benefit more people.

Addressing Inequities

Although knowledge about the sources of social injustice is important for understanding some of the obstacles people encounter as they pursue their occupational goals, that knowledge needs to be translated into action (Arthur, 2018b, 2019a). Incorporating social justice into everyday language should not be mistaken for actively engaging in social justice advocacy. Professional conversations are important as they can be the starting point for identifying key issues and developing strategies. Dialogue can also be used strategically as a starting point for addressing the systemic and structural barriers that many of our clients and members of the public face in their daily lives. Beyond identifying barriers, practitioners are encouraged to consider client strengths, available resources, and untapped opportunities.

> *Exploring constraints and opportunities.* Explore how the properties of pathways (e.g., accessibility, mobility, prestige, extrinsic rewards) may be affected by client characteristics (e.g., gender, social circumstances, cultural identity) and context (e.g., historical time and place). Discuss meeting challenges. Engage in relevant advocacy. (Bakshi & Fialho, 2019, p. 40)

Career practitioners empower clients by providing education and information to support their career planning and decision making. For example, individuals may be trying to make occupational decisions without adequate information about current jobs and requirements, how their capabilities might be utilized in a fuller range of occupations, or what training and resources might be available. "Consider the role of LMI [labour market information] in your practice. Is it central or peripheral? Empowering clients with high-quality information can be a powerful stimulus that helps clients overcome structural barriers" (Bimrose, 2019b, p. 62). Social advocacy includes using our professional knowledge to increase the knowledge of our clients and empowering them to use that information in a guided process. "Counsellors can be facilitators and cheerleaders for their clients, encouraging them to build resilience, to become cognizant of their strengths, and to advocate for themselves" (Tang, 2019, p. 410).

You can work with clients directly or use your advocacy skills to improve the conditions that people face in their employment and/or community contexts. "Career counselling only is one type of intervention. Advocacy might make a big difference with clients, on their behalf, and for others" (Arthur, 2019b, p. 30). If conditions external to the individual could be changed, an individual might no longer feel distressed and could thrive in the situation. To illustrate: Imagine a client who is struggling in their work context because they feel pressured to increase their productivity with longer hours and with limited support. Helping this client to improve their coping skills could be an intervention focus, but it would likely not change the conditions in their workplace. In contrast, an intervention might involve coaching towards the client's self-advocacy. This might entail providing information about workers' employment rights and/or exploring ways to garner support in the workplace to address the work conditions. Discussing safety consideration is recommended in discussions with clients to address power issues and potential ramifications of advocating for change in the workplace. At a different level, practitioners may also engage in social advocacy to promote change in the contexts of work. From the perspective of changing the conditions of work, "social advocacy is essential in advancing a more just context for work and for personal development" (Blustein, Duffy et al., 2019, p. 72).

Using Our Professional Voices

As noted in the previous examples, career practitioners can use their professional knowledge and skills to advocate for social justice. Even though, at times, you may not feel like you have a lot of power, your training and experience do afford you certain advantages. You might already have considerable knowledge and experience with systems and services that can be leveraged to promote individual and social change. In some roles, you might act as a knowledge broker to help your clients navigate the complexities of their life circumstances and/or you might empower clients by providing access to new resources. You could also use your knowledge directly with clients to help them develop skills for self-advocacy.

> **Advocacy.** *Intervening on behalf of your client can be regarded as contentious. For example, contacting an employer on behalf of a client (with their full permission and knowledge) can be an effective method to secure a selection interview for a client. It may also be necessary to accompany the client. Consider other ways in which this approach to practice might enhance outcomes for the client.* (Bimrose, 2019b, p. 62)

The main point is that there are multiple ways to engage in advocacy, such as building community capacity, improving access to resources, and working together with other professionals. Advocacy may involve developing new programs and services or revising existing offerings to increase access or capacity. Consider carefully who is engaged in partnerships that determine the nature of career services and whose voices inform strategies for responding to the needs of individuals, groups, and communities. Remember the point introduced earlier in this chapter about one of the ways to conceptualize and practice social justice – engage people as coparticipants in determining their priority issues and relevant solutions.

To reiterate a key point: not everyone is afforded the same social advantages and it is important to "provide positive social advocacy" (Pope, 2019, p. 346). Advocacy for career service provision includes consideration of who has access to services and who has been overlooked. Actions can be taken to "identify the measures, information, or resources that help [people] to access those services" (Picard et al., 2019, p. 316).

> **More voices count.** *Collectively speak out for your profession so as not to individualize the challenges and the effort needed, which could require an excessive amount of energy.* (Viviers, 2019, p. 431)

Career practitioners can use their professional voices in multiple ways to advocate for social justice. Although you can do so individually, sharing practices and mobilizing the collective efforts of colleagues and allies can be energizing and have greater impact. You might also consider ways to engage with your professional associations to define, represent, and defend the work of career practitioners (Viviers, 2019, p. 431).

Conclusion

Unfortunately, many individuals face multiple barriers in their careers because not everyone needs the same resources and there can be restrictions for accessing opportunities and services. Career practitioners can play an important role in promoting equitable access to educational and employment systems. Your individual and collective efforts can address social inequities and provide options for people to enhance their career development. Joining with other professionals is a way to stay energized and supported in the process of advocating for social and structural change.

Career Development Practice Incorporates Social Justice Advocacy: Reflection Questions

Revisit the personal vignette you created in Chapter 1. Use the following questions to apply the content of this chapter to your vignette. Consider your personal experiences of career development and/or your role as a career practitioner:

1. How have privilege and/or social disadvantage influenced your career development?
2. What are your experiences with work, paid or unpaid (e.g., employment, caregiving, volunteering)?
3. How might you collaborate with clients to help them address any inequities related to their career issues?
4. What social-justice-advocacy roles or actions interest you?
5. Do you have any concerns about advocating for social justice? If so, with whom might you discuss those concerns?
6. In what ways could you use your professional power, as an individual or collectively with other professionals, to advocate for social justice?

Chapter 9

Career Development Practice Involves Collaboration With Other Professionals

Collaborating with other professionals, including peers, expanded professional networks, and members of multidisciplinary teams enhances your services to clients and your own lifelong learning to stay current. The focus of Chapter 9 is to:

- Emphasize the importance of professional collaboration, both within the career development sector and on multidisciplinary teams
- Encourage innovation and sharing through ongoing professional development activities
- Highlight the need for lifelong learning to effectively integrate emerging theories and models into practice

As you read, pause periodically to reflect on the personal vignette that you created in Chapter 1. Questions for further reflection are listed at the end of this chapter.

Collaboration as an Essential Skill for Contemporary Practice: It Takes a Village

Careers do not develop in isolation; career development practice, therefore, requires an integrative effort to engage others in supporting your work with your clients. In Chapter 5, we described how "it takes a village" to develop a career. This chapter applies the adage to your career and practice, identifying collaboration with other professionals as an essential skill for career development practitioners. Such collaboration includes building professional networks, working on multidisciplinary teams, and a continuous commitment to your own ongoing professional development.

Effective career development practice is not an isolated moment of service provision, but rather integrates lifelong interventions and supports. Career development professionals need to work strategically and cooperatively with their colleagues, the employer community, and funders (Canadian Career Development Foundation, 2021b; Herr, 2000; Pasolli & Cummings, 2021). With many clients, the need for collaboration will further extend to their family members, educators, and members of multidisciplinary professional teams.

In current career practice, many funders require community partnerships to ensure a holistic and comprehensive approach to service delivery (Bimrose & Goddard, 2021). Such partnerships are intended to reduce redundancy of services and also to strengthen access to support for clients with diverse needs. Even if not mandated, collaboration makes good sense—maximizing opportunities to utilize our professional strengths, minimizing redundancy, sharing resources, and providing wraparound support to clients as they navigate increasingly complex career transitions (McKenzie & Goddard, 2021).

Professional interconnectedness can reveal to us our own blind spots—to borrow another adage, we simply "don't know what we don't know." The Johari Window model suggests that our blind spots are reduced through relationships with others (Robertson, 2009). Our professional colleagues, supervisors, mentors, and those with whom we consult can hold a mirror up for us to recognize our gaps in knowledge or self-awareness so that we are continuously learning how to better serve our clients (Thomson et al., 2021).

In the four stages of competence model (Adams, n.d.), we all begin in *unconscious incompetence*; there are things we are not doing well, but we do not yet realize that, so we think we are managing just fine. Sometimes we stumble into the stage of *conscious incompetence* where we are fully aware that we do not know what to do. Although most of our ethical codes caution us against working outside of our boundaries of competence (e.g., Canadian Career Development Foundation, 2021c; International Association for Educational and Vocational Guidance, 2017), sometimes we find clients' issues surfacing that we just did not see coming or we become aware of a cultural difference that we had never previously encountered. Collaboration with colleagues and others supports the sometimes-awkward shift from *conscious competence*, where you are learning something new, to *unconscious competence*, the place where you have fully integrated a new competency into your practice.

Both the Johari Window and the four stages of competence models highlight the relationship between professional interconnectedness and lifelong learning. These two themes will be more fully explored in the sections that follow.

Career Practitioners and Professional Networks

Career development practitioners work within complex and interconnected systems (Bronfenbrenner, 2000; McMahon, 2019a). As described in Chapter 3, your working relationship with individual clients and groups is foundational to the success of your practice. However, the support you offer your clients may involve interacting with other systems that impact them, such as educational institutions, employers, funders, and other community service providers. Even within a single community agency, there may be a team of career practitioners working together to provide services; this could include a colleague staffing the drop-in resource room, an intake worker, a case manager, a job developer, several workshop facilitators, a resumé writer and/or interview coach, and supervisors and managers (Bezanson et al., 2009; Pickerell & Neault, 2012). In smaller agencies, however, one career development practitioner may fulfill all or most of these roles. One's context may determine levels of professional interconnectedness. Large teams may be quite self-contained, with the capacity even to offer in-house foundational training and ongoing professional development. Smaller teams, however, will benefit from larger interconnected professional networks. Such networks can include other service providers to whom you can refer your clients and also provide sources of information and professional development for your own ongoing learning. Amundson (2019) cautioned us about working too independently. Working on our own may not only lead to blind spots but also limit our creativity, contribute to burnout, and, in some cases, completely waste time.

Viviers (2019) emphasized the links between work and mental health. Clearly, this is an important consideration in your work with clients. However, you are workers yourselves; attending to your own workloads, working conditions, and work relationships is important to your own mental health, well-being, and develop-

> **Be collaborative.** Are you trying to do too much by yourself? Use your colleagues for collaboration and support. (Amundson, 2019, p. 9)

ment as professionals. Viviers encourages you to engage in conversations with your colleagues and supervisors, thereby facilitating opportunities to learn from each other and creating healthier workplaces for all. Recognizing your capacity limits to do your job well without burning out, Viviers also advised career practitioners to "advocate for resources. Join forces with other professionals to advocate for the hiring of support services to free up time for the main functions of guidance work" (p. 431). This, of course, echoed Amundson's (2019) compelling question: "Are you trying to do too much by yourself?"

Beyond seeking support from your immediate work teams, consider joining one (or several!) of the many professional associations within the career development sector—locally, nationally, and/or internationally. Some associations have formal structures and offer certification for career development practitioners. Within Canada, for example, many pro-

> **Share your vision.** Discuss your vision with other members of your work community to make them aware of it. Also, draw on examples from the structure of other workplaces (Viviers, 2019, p. 431).

vincial career development associations offer certification programs, and work on a national certification is underway (Canadian Career Development Foundation, n.d.). Other associations and organizations serve as advocates for the profession, though lobbying policymakers and funders (e.g., Association of Service Providers for Employability and Career Training, 2022), or provide networking opportunities through conferences and other professional development events (e.g., the annual Cannexus conference, https://cannexus.ceric.ca/). There are similar examples across the world, so we encourage you to seek out local and national conferences within your own country contexts, as well as such international organizations as the International Association for Educational Guidance (https://iaevg.com/), Euroguidance (https://euroguidance.eu), or the Asia Pacific Career Development Association (https://apcda.wildapricot.org/). Many associations produce publications to help their members stay current. These publications come in various formats—from informal blogs and e-newsletters to published magazines, academic peer-reviewed journals, relevant books, and other career development resources.

Aside from simply consuming such resources, consider contributing to the professional development of your peers. This book, for example, is the result of professional collaboration. It began with casual communication at various local and international conferences, then grew into the project that resulted in *Career Theories and Models at Work: Ideas for Practice* (Arthur et al., 2019), the 43-chapter book from which the practice points in this current book were all drawn. *Career Theories and Models at Work* comprised contributions from authors across four continents, and most of the connections with the contributing authors had been formed over several years through networking at conferences and professional development events around the world.

> **Mobilize your skills.** *Use your communication skills and network to support the professional interests of guidance counsellors, and to keep your sense of humour* (Viviers, 2019, p. 431).

Multidisciplinary Networks

In addition to important career development networks, locally and internationally, collaboration with professionals from outside of the career development sector will sometimes be required to effectively serve your clients. Reflecting on the complex systems described in Bronfenbrenner's (2000) model, what other professionals do you have, and/or need, in your network? As noted in codes of ethics (e.g., Canadian Career Development Foundation, 2021c), signed release-of-information forms would be needed to discuss specific clients with their family members, family physicians, instructors, addiction counsellors, social workers, employers, or other significant people who are influencing their career development. However, sometimes you can leverage your networks for advocacy purposes or simply to gather generic information that will help you to better serve your diverse clientele.

Viviers (2019) offered a reminder of the strength in strategic alliances—within the career development sector and beyond:

> **Create professional alliances.** Alliances can help you to stand your ground in multidisciplinary teams, to inform colleagues about your profession and the role you play in your organization, or to claim the conditions or resources required for the professional practice of counselling in your workplace. (p. 431)

Your professional networks will be vital to your success as a career practitioner. Sometimes you may find yourself as the lone voice with career development expertise on a team with other professionals. You will need allies, from the career development sector and far beyond, to effectively advocate for what you need to be successful in your role and, ultimately, to ensure the success of your clients.

Professional Development: A Lifelong Commitment

Continuing to develop professional competencies is an ethical responsibility. It is also essential to effective career development practice within increasingly complex and constantly changing contexts. One of the foundational competencies for career practitioners is to apply career development theories and models (Canadian Career Development Foundation, 2021a; International Association for Educational and Vocational Guidance, 2018). This can be an important area of ongoing professional development. As you add new theories and their related interventions to your toolkits, seek out professional development opportunities to strengthen your competency in applying those theories within your practice. For example, Osborn, Dozier, Bullock Yowell, and their colleagues (2019) acknowledged that research on cognitive information processing (CIP) continues; they advised practitioners to "stay current on CIP research" (p. 306) and pointed practitioners to a website where the most recent research is posted. Similarly, Sheu and Wang (2019), in discussing social cognitive career theory, recognized that "given its comprehensive nature, SCCT may appear daunting at first glance. Career counsellors should familiarize themselves with its variables and tenets in order to be effective in applying the theory" (p. 389). Spangar (2019), in writing about sociodynamic career counselling, took a similar stance, encouraging practitioners to "familiarize yourself with sociodynamic methods. Read some of Vance Peavy's original work" (p. 400), mentioning specific foundational resources developed by the original theorist.

Clearly, there is a wide range of professional development activities that practitioners can engage in to strengthen competency in translating theory into practice. It is particularly exciting and enlightening to learn directly from theorists and those who have developed the models and frameworks that guide career development practice. Such opportunities may come through reading academic research articles, books, or less formal publications, such as blogs, newsletters, e-zines, and social media posts. Attending conference presentations, including keynote addresses, is another way to learn directly from the people behind the theories and models that you use. You can also find many videos, audio recordings, or podcasts by theorists freely available online. Many theorists offer training sessions—register for such opportunities for in-depth learning if you have the chance.

Beyond learning about specific theories and models, you might also consider integrative professional development opportunities such as courses, webinars, or workshops that help to bring a variety of relevant theories to life.

> *Adopt cross-training as part of your life-long learning strategy. If you are working with increasing diversity, the sources you typically use may not address all of the issues you face. Reading outside your field may provide helpful insight into thoughts or activities that others have used to address some of the issues you are working with. For example, some helpful areas to read about include creativity and imagination, cross-cultural communication, posttraumatic growth, neurocognition and brain plasticity, and story.* (Poehnell, 2019, p. 326)

Finally, we encourage you to contribute to the professional development of other career practitioners and career influencers, including employers and educators. Spangar (2019) suggested that you "come up with your own methods and communicate them to your colleagues. Use your wisdom to improvise and to be creative in the counselling process" (p. 400). We hope you will share your experiences and expertise widely, perhaps by presenting at conferences, contributing to forums, or writing about what's working well in your practice. We look forward to learning from each of you.

Conclusion

This takes us full circle—in the beginning of this chapter, we introduced the notion that "it takes a village." Collaboration with other professionals, within the career development sector and on multidisciplinary teams, contributes to effective and theoretically grounded career development practice. Continuing to learn, and sharing what you learn, will keep your practice current, enrich the practice of your colleagues, and maximize the effectiveness of your work with diverse clients and communities.

Career Development Practice Involves Collaboration With Other Professionals: Reflection Questions

Revisit the personal vignette you created in Chapter 1. Use the following questions to apply the content of this chapter to your vignette. Consider how you may need to stretch beyond your current competencies and resources to effectively address the complexity of the vignette you have been examining.

1. Who is in your "village" of professional connections? How has collaboration with other professionals strengthened your practice and helped you to stay current?
2. What professional networks and/or associations are you part of? What other professional networks and/or associations might it benefit you to join?
3. Beyond the career development sector, which other professions do you consult with?
4. What advantages have you experienced from being part of multidisciplinary teams?
5. What gaps have you identified within your multidisciplinary network? How might you strategically connect with others to fill those gaps?
6. How can you nurture your professional network to keep it sustainable?
7. What professional development goals do you have to strengthen your competency in theory-informed practice for the next month? Six months? Year? Five years?

Chapter 10

Implications for Career Theories and Models in Practice

This chapter summarizes our learning about developing eight practice principles to support career practitioners to use theory-based practice. The purpose of Chapter 10 is to:

- Draw connections between the eight practice principles described in the previous chapters
- Overview five core practices for career practitioners synthesized from the practice principles
- Introduce the Career Practice Reflection Guide
- Encourage ongoing professional learning about theory–practice connections

In the preface to this book, we noted how much we learned from editing and reviewing the text of our first book, *Career Theories and Models at Work: Ideas for Practice* (Arthur et al., 2019). It was from our individual and collective learning that we decided to explore more deeply the connections between the chapters in that book, particularly the practice points offered by the chapter authors. Our learning has continued as we analyzed the practice points and synthesized eight practice principles, presented in Chapters 2 to 9. Now, in the final stage of this project, we have reflected on what we learned from writing about the practice principles and how we might further integrate them into a meaningful framework for career practice.

To recap, the foundations of this book are the words of the many contributors to *Career Theories and Models at Work: Ideas for Practice* (Arthur et al., 2019). What is unique about the practice points is that they were derived from specific theories and models of career development. We wanted to emphasize the importance of practitioners gaining knowledge about theories and models and selecting approaches that make sense to them and that inform the ways that they engage in practice. The chapter authors' contributions, in particular the practice points they listed at the end of their chapters, stimulated the synthesis that we conducted to identify the foundations of "what all practitioners need to know" and provided the chapter structure for this book. This important and innovative work extrapolated core knowledge from the practice points to provide career practitioners with the eight practice principles that are elaborated in the previous chapters:

1. Career development practice integrates practitioner reflection.
2. Career development practice is built on relationships.
3. Career development practice involves collaboration with clients.
4. Career development practice requires customization.
5. Career development practice is based on theory.
6. Career development practice occurs in cultural contexts.
7. Career development practice incorporates social justice advocacy.
8. Career development practice involves collaboration with other professionals.

Although we have written about these practice principles in separate chapters, they often overlap, and many of the practice principles are linked. Each of the chapters provides detailed examples and explanations, but we hope that you will consider the interconnections between the practice principles and the specific points and quotes highlighted. As you become more familiar with new ideas, or review points that you already use, consider what you want to emphasize, combine, or integrate in the approaches that you use. We personally took up this challenge when we pondered about our learning across the eight principles to inform our career practice.

Five Core Practices for Career Practitioners

As we further reflected on the eight practice principles, we identified five core practices to guide the work of all career practitioners, regardless of their theoretical orientations, their specific roles, the populations they serve, or the stages of career development that they support. To work ethically and effectively within the complexity of today's diverse contexts, career practitioners need to *reflect, connect, contextualize, customize,* and *collaborate* (see Figure 1).

1. Reflect

As we noted in Chapter 2, the notion of reflexivity, or being a reflective practitioner, is not new, but is generally considered foundational in professional practice. Reflection was mentioned explicitly in the practice points across one-third of the chapters in the original book and was certainly implied in others. We have emphasized that reflection requires being intentional about theory-practice connections.

As career practitioners, you are encouraged to reflect deeply and often—on yourselves, your practice, the uniqueness of each of your clients (including their

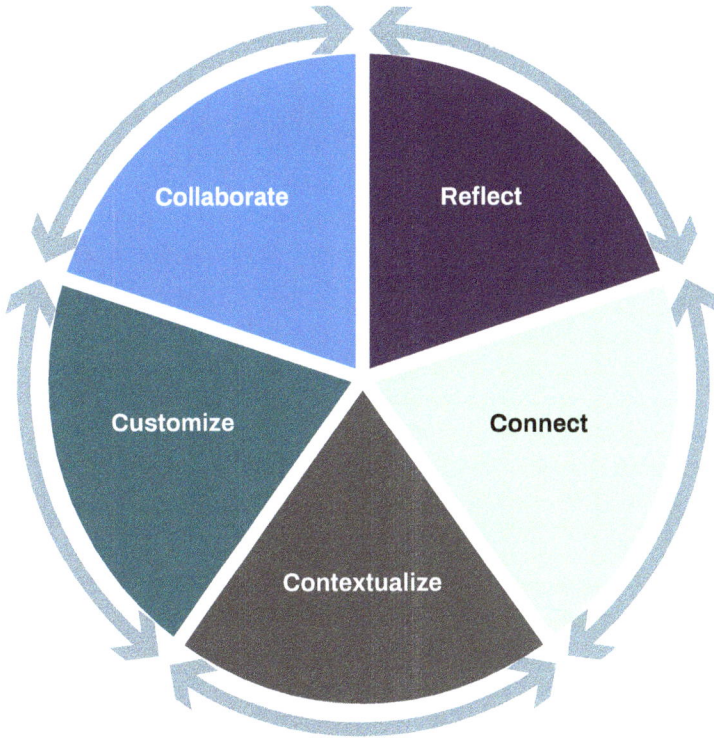

Figure 1: Five core practices

cultures and contexts), your own motivation to do the work you do and, also, the motivation of your clients to take the next step on their career journeys. You are encouraged to engage in reflection as you evaluate the progress of your work with clients and, also, as you consider next steps in your own professional development.

Making reflection the foundation of your practice will ensure that your practice remains current, relevant, targeted, and efficient. As emphasized throughout this book, and as the focus of Chapter 6, we encourage you to reflect on your selection of career theories and models and to track their applications through theory-informed practice. Reflection *before* seeing a client will help you to be curious and to prepare meaningful questions, interventions, and referral sources. Reflection *while* you are engaged with your client will build in pauses to check your own biases, assumptions, and sense of how to proceed. Engaging your client in a reflective process will help you to stay aligned in terms of goals and direction for collaborative next steps. Engaging in reflection *after* your sessions will help you to identify what worked well, what did not, and what may still need to be addressed. Such post-session reflexivity can also help you with a bigger picture perspective of your work together and a better understanding of what else may be going on within your client's context.

2. Connect

Reflection is an ongoing process and so is connecting. Fundamental to effective career practice is a strong connection between career practitioners and clients. This connection is often referred to in building a strong working alliance, the focus of Chapters 3 and 4. These chapters highlight the importance of quality practitioner–client relationships. Effective partnerships with your clients are built on trusting and respectful working alliances. Building an effective practitioner–client relationship is not a single step in the process of working with clients. Rather, it is something that needs to be attended to at all stages of the collaborative work being done together by practitioners and clients.

Nurturing a quality relationship involves creating a safe space for clients to tell their stories, facilitating rather than directing, and being guided by your clients as to what might work best work for them, by listening to the client's story and starting with what clients give you. Quality practitioner–client relationships strengthen over time from consistently being attended to. Each client is unique in terms of their personal characteristics, cultures, contexts, circumstances, motivation, readiness for change, and level of personal agency.

Attending to clients' uniqueness necessitates personalized interventions by practitioners. With this point in mind, Chapter 6 considered the need to connect with the theoretical base of your work, Chapter 7 discussed the need to consider the cultural contexts of practice, and Chapter 5 discussed the need to customize practice to suit clients' needs rather than taking a formulaic approach. Customizing practice helps clients to feel that they matter and that you as the career practitioner are responsive to their needs; this, in turn, strengthens the working alliance.

3. Contextualize

People's lives are embedded in unique contexts. In Chapter 7, we invited you to consider your personal life contexts and the influences on your career development, such as how your life contexts might be similar or different from the background experiences, strengths, barriers, and resources in the lives of the clients you serve. Chapter 8 contained practice points about ensuring assessment and intervention processes incorporate people's experience of privilege and/or oppression and their access to education and employment opportunities. While acknowledging that there are multiple career pathways, you can assist people to leverage available resources and collaborate with them on ways to address structural or social barriers.

In taking a holistic approach to people's career development, you can explore people's life roles, including their views about paid and unpaid work. As you listen carefully to clients' stories, you can gain understanding about the experiences and relationships that clients consider to be most influential for their past, present, and future career development. Messages received from family, peers, or media can provide useful clues about peoples' values and beliefs that are relevant for understanding their career-related behaviour. Also, you can acknowledge the connections between work, mental health, and workplace cultures, and inquire about people's sense of belonging and their feelings of being "on-track" or "off-track" in their lives.

As emphasized in Chapter 8, you can use your professional knowledge and connections to support change directly with individuals or with other systems. You might advocate for greater access to career development services, address a specific barrier an individual faces or groups of people commonly experience, or review existing programs or services to consider who is included or excluded. Career practitioners work within the contexts of their employment organizations; this means responding to funding and service mandates while also continually working to improve access to resources and services — for you and for your clients.

4. Customize

Fuelled by reflection and informed by a deep connection with your clients and attention to their contexts and cultures, the next core practice is to customize your career services. With a design-thinking approach, as described in Chapter 5, such customization could occur on multiple levels. With individual clients, you could adjust the level and style of language you are using to be more age-appropriate or to better accommodate language learners or people with lower literacy. For example, you may incorporate technology to a greater or lesser degree, depending on the digital literacy levels of your clients and/or their comfort with technology. You may adjust the pace of your work together, based on client readiness, motivation, or capacity for change. You may introduce assistive technologies or other accommodations for clients with differing abilities. You may engage clients in memorable, experiential learning activities. You may also customize by drawing from other disciplines such as counselling, psychology, or adult education.

Customization may also occur at the program level. For example, there may be synergies and efficiencies in working with clients in a group rather than only individually. You may increase your reach by offering some services virtually, or in a hybrid format, rather than only in person. You may consider modularizing your program so that individuals can benefit from the specific components that they need (or are ready for) rather than being required to participate in all or nothing. For existing groups, or for individuals within a specific cultural context, you may need to adjust graphic design elements, case examples, activities, and discussion prompts to ensure that they are culturally appropriate and relevant.

Customization may also occur at a policy level. Consider advocating for the programs and services that the people you serve really need. You could use design thinking to customize cost-effective and efficacious prototypes in a continuous-improvement approach to career development.

5. Collaborate

The adage "it takes a village" was used in Chapters 5 and 9. As highlighted in Chapter 3, building a solid working alliance requires more than simply *connecting* with clients.

Fostering *collaboration* with your clients can enhance their agency, empower them to make personally meaningful choices, and facilitate clients' claiming (or reclaiming) their autonomy over significant life decisions. As previously noted, considering context is also important. Collaborating with clients provides the space for them to serve as the experts on their own lives and contextual realities.

Collaboration can also extend beyond the practitioner–client relationship to include engaging with family members, employers, educators, and other career influencers and individuals who may impact (or be impacted by) your clients' career decisions. There are long-term benefits to helping your clients activate their own "village" of supports that will be there for them long after your professional work together is done. As noted in the discussion about contextualization, it is important to identify the people and life roles that are relevant for your clients.

As emphasized in Chapter 9, collaboration with other professionals is also important. Rather than working alone or in professional silos (and, unfortunately, sometimes at cross-purposes), collaborating with colleagues can maximize the benefits to your clients of a holistic wraparound approach to career/life development.

As highlighted in Chapter 8, career practitioners are also called to advocacy roles. This, too, can involve collaboration—with colleagues, organizations, communities, and governments—to address inequities, social injustices, and oppression. Collaboration through your professional associations might be useful for mobilizing collective action and offering evidence and solutions to policy issues.

Finally, collaboration can be key to your ongoing professional development—and to the lifelong career development of your clients. In isolation, we tend not to be aware of what we don't know. In communities of collaboration, however, we can learn from each other and share our emerging perspectives.

Where to From Here?

In this book, we have encouraged you to use a personal vignette or a case vignette from your practice as a reference point for reflection. We have also developed a new *Career Practice Reflection Guide*, found at the end of this chapter, that lists the reflection questions introduced in Chapters 2–9. The guide is something that you can reference in everyday practice. You might want to focus on a specific practice principle or on individual questions or prompts across the practice principles to help guide your reflections in future practice. Remember, the practice tool is based on theoretically driven practice points, and we encourage you to consider how you are connecting theory to practice.

Whether you are new to the field of career development practice or a seasoned practitioner, ongoing reflection can help you to strengthen or sharpen the intentional ways that you select and use the techniques and practice points derived from career theories and models. For example, if there was a pause in your work, could you explain *what* you are doing, *how* you are approaching practice, and *why* you are taking that approach, with reference to a career theory or model? The suggestions in this chapter may offer you new ideas about how you can strengthen your career practice. In essence, we hope that you will use the *Career Practice Reflection Guide* that we have developed, along with the elaborated chapter contents, to inform an ethical and intentional approach to career practice.

Throughout the book, we have emphasized the importance of ongoing, continuous learning and professional development. Referring to the reflection process initiated in Chapter 1, you might take the time now to consider your learning journey in reading this book. What were your highlights as you reviewed the subsequent chapters? What content surprised you? What areas of knowledge or skill development seemed familiar or new to you? What are your curiosities for future learning and development? We hope that you will continue the process of reflection that was introduced in the book, in order to target specific learning goals now and in your future practice.

In this book, we have looked across the practice points offered by the authors of theories and models to determine the foundations of career practice. In other words, we hope that you will use the eight practice principles and five core practices to guide your work and to enhance theory-practice connections. Extending from the practice principle discussed in Chapter 2, reflexive practice is an ongoing process and one of the five core career practices — it is foundational to all aspects of your professional work. Grounded in reflexive practice, you will be well-positioned to connect deeply with your clients, to contextualize their career concerns, to customize effective interventions and approaches, and to collaborate with colleagues and all relevant stakeholders.

In summary, this book provides suggestions about ways that you can deepen your practice, through selecting and focusing on specific practice principles (i.e., *what* you do), reflecting back to the theoretical foundations of those principles (i.e., *why* you do what you do), and integrating the five core practices (i.e., *how* you do what you do). We encourage you to discuss and incorporate the practice principles into case conceptualization, session reviews, or formal or informal supervision practices. We also encourage you to share your ideas to inform practice innovations. We hope that the content of the book chapters has sparked your curiosity and commitment to continued professional learning about theory-informed practice.

Career Practice Reflection Guide©*

Nancy Arthur, Roberta Borgen, Mary McMahon

This *Career Practice Reflection Guide* represents the culmination of two projects designed to make theory more accessible to career practitioners. The first project concluded with the publication of *Career Theories and Models at Work: Ideas for Practice* (Arthur et al., 2019). That book contained 43 chapters, each of which concluded with a set of practice points designed to assist practitioners to better understand and apply the theory or model. The second project evolved from the first and concluded with the book, *Practice Principles: Career Theories and Models at Work* (Arthur et al., 2024). This second book focused on the practice points collected during the first project, which we synthesized into the following practice principles:

1. Career development practice integrates practitioner reflection.
2. Career development practice is built on relationships.
3. Career development practice involves collaboration with clients.
4. Career development practice requires customization.
5. Career development practice is based on theory.
6. Career development practice occurs in cultural contexts.
7. Career development practice incorporates social justice advocacy.
8. Career development practice involves collaboration with other professionals.

Each practice principle was the subject of a separate chapter in the book. At the end of each of those chapters, we posed reflection questions to assist readers to better understand and apply the principle. This *Career Practice Reflection Guide* is a collation of those reflection questions.

There are many ways to use the Guide, whether you are a student of career development, a beginning practitioner, an experienced practitioner, or a provider of career development practitioner training. For example, you might consider a practice scenario with a client, past or present, as the reference point for your reflection. You might also consider your own career development as the reference point for your reflection. You might determine professional development goals to strengthen your competency in theory-informed practice. You could use the guide in a comprehensive way, to reflect on each of the practice principles, or selectively, to focus on one or more of the principles. You could use this reflection guide on your own or with colleagues. You might select some of the reflection questions for supervision discussions. The reflection process and the content related to the practice principles could also supplement curriculum, training, or professional development seminars. These are some examples of ways that you might engage in reflection to enhance your understanding of the eight principles that underpin theory-informed career practice.

Source: Arthur, N., Borgen, R., & McMahon, M. (2024). *Practice principles: Career theories and models at work.* CERIC.

Career development practice integrates practitioner reflection.

1. What experiences have been key influences in your personal career development?
2. How did gender influence your pursuit of occupations or the occupations your family members pursued and selected?
3. How did aspects of your identity other than gender (e.g., ethnicity, social class, religion, ability), or their intersections, influence your pursuit of occupations?
4. What were the views of your family and friends on issues such as the types of jobs considered desirable, unemployment, and career success? How did their views influence you?
5. How do you engage in reflective practice currently?
6. In what ways could you strengthen your engagement with reflective practice?

Career development practice is built on relationships.

7. Think of a time when you had an effective practitioner–client relationship What did you do to facilitate the relationship?
8. How do you understand your role in establishing effective practitioner–client relationships?
9. What steps would you take with a client to build an effective relationship?
10. How would you explain the practitioner–client relationship to a colleague?
11. How would you explain the practitioner–client relationship to a client?
12. How would you explain the working alliance to a colleague?
13. How would you explain to a client their role in the working alliance?

Career development practice involves collaboration with clients.

14. How has attending to the unique personal characteristics and contexts of your clients helped you to foster collaborative relationships with them?
15. What strategies have you found most effective in facilitating a strengths-based approach?
16. Reflect on a time when a client seemed particularly motivated to collaborate with you in working towards a career goal. What fuelled that motivation?
17. Reflect on a time when a client seemed particularly unmotivated or seemed to lose motivation. What contributed to that? Were you able to work together to turn it around? If yes, how? If not, what were the challenges?
18. Identify three to five factors that may be impacting a client's readiness for change. What types of support/scaffolding might help your client to engage in a change process?

Career development practice requires customization.

19. How do the levels of language you use in speaking and writing facilitate your clients' career development?
20. What types of experiential learning activities have you introduced to your clients?
21. What might make your clients' learning more memorable?
22. As you reflect on clients' needs for customization and accommodation, what are you inspired to add to your own career development toolkit?
23. What strategies might you use to promote your clients' personal agency and autonomy?
24. How can you support clients to respond effectively to changes impacting their goals and plans?
25. Consider one client's "village" of supports. Who else might be invited to contribute to this client's career development? How might they offer support?

Career development practice is based on theory.

26. How could your career (e.g., stages, influences, experiences) be explained by each of the career theories or models most familiar to you?
27. In what ways do the career theories and models most familiar to you complement or contradict each other when applied to your career?
28. Are there aspects of your career that you feel are not accounted for by the career theories and models most familiar to you? If so, read about another theory or model you are less familiar with and identify ways in which it might apply to your own career.
29. How would you explain the career theory or model that most informs your work to a colleague?
30. Identify three career theories or models that are less familiar to you and reflect on how they could guide your work with a specific client.
31. How would you explain to a client how you understand their concerns theoretically?

Career development practice occurs in cultural contexts.

32. How do the career theories or models that you use account for the diversity in people's life contexts and career pathways?
33. What approaches could you use to learn about your clients' cultural worldviews, such as individualism and collectivism?
34. How do you incorporate clients' relationships in discussions about their presenting career issues?
35. What does the phrase *clients are the experts on their own lives* mean to you?
36. How would you respond when a client is pursuing a pathway to a career goal that you feel might not be the best choice?

Source: Arthur, N., Borgen, R., & McMahon, M. (2024). *Practice principles: Career theories and models at work*. CERIC.

37. Reflect on the workplace cultures at organizations where you have been employed. How might the contexts in which you have personal experience be similar or different to the organizational contexts where your clients work or want to work?

Career development practice incorporates social justice advocacy.

38. How have privilege and/or social disadvantage influenced your career development?
39. What are your experiences with work, paid or unpaid, (e.g., employment, caregiving, volunteering)?
40. How might you collaborate with clients to help them address any inequities related to their career issues?
41. What social-justice-advocacy roles or actions interest you?
42. Do you have any concerns about advocating for social justice? If so, with whom might you discuss those concerns?
43. In what ways could you use your professional power, as an individual or collectively with other professionals, to advocate for social justice?

Career development practice involves collaboration with other professionals.

44. Who is in your "village" of professional connections? How has collaboration with other professionals strengthened your practice and helped you to stay current?
45. What professional networks and/or associations are you part of? What other professional networks and/or associations might it benefit you to join?
46. Beyond the career development sector, which other professions do you consult with?
47. What advantages have you experienced from being part of multidisciplinary teams?
48. What gaps have you identified within your multidisciplinary network? How might you strategically connect with others to fill those gaps?
49. How can you nurture your professional network to keep it sustainable?

References

Arthur, N., Neault, R., & McMahon, M. (2019). *Career theories and models at work: Ideas for practice*. CERIC.

Arthur, N., Borgen, R., & McMahon, M. (2024). *Practice principles: Career theories and models at work*. CERIC.

* **Distribution of the *Career Practice Reflection Guide*, including photocopying or electronic distribution, requires acknowledgement of the authors and book reference.**

Source: Arthur, N., Borgen, R., & McMahon, M. (2024). *Practice principles: Career theories and models at work*. CERIC.

References

Adams, L. (n.d.). *Learning a new skill is easier said than done*. Gordon Training International. https://www.gordontraining.com/free-workplace-articles/learning-a-new-skill-is-easier-said-than-done/

Ali, S. R., & Brown, S. D. (2017). Integration of theory, research, and practice: Using our tools to address challenging times. In J. P. Sampson, E. Bullock-Yowell, V. C. Dozier, D. S. Osborn, & J. G. Lenz (Eds.), *Integrating theory, research, and practice in vocational psychology: Current status and future directions* (pp. 73–76). Florida State University. https://doi.org/10.17125/svp2016.ch6

Amundson, N. E. (2018). *Active engagement* (4th ed). Ergon Communications

Amundson, N. (2019). Active engagement: Answering the call for imagination. In N. Arthur, R. Neault, & M. McMahon (Eds.), *Career theories and models at work: Ideas for practice* (pp. 1–9). CERIC.

Aravind, S., & Arulmani, G. (2019). Understanding the career development of children with dyslexia: The cultural preparation process model of career development. In N. Arthur, R. Neault, & M. McMahon (Eds.), *Career theories and models at work: Ideas for practice* (pp. 11–19). CERIC.

Arthur, N. (2017). Constructivist approaches to career counseling: A culture-infused approach. In M. McMahon (Ed.), *Career counselling: Constructivist approaches* (2nd ed., pp. 54–64). Routledge.

Arthur, N. (2018a). Infusing culture and social justice in ethical practices with all clients. In N. Arthur (Ed.), *Counselling in cultural contexts: Identities and social justice* (pp. 3–28). Springer.

Arthur, N. (2018b. Culture-infused counselling: Moving forward with applied activism and advocacy. In N. Arthur (Ed.), *Counselling in cultural contexts: Identities and social justice* (pp. 383–406). Springer.

Arthur, N. (2019a). Career development theory and practice: A culture-infused perspective. In N. Arthur & M. McMahon (Eds.), *Contemporary theories of career development: International perspectives* (pp. 180–194). Routledge.

Arthur, N. (2019b). Culture-infused career counselling: Connecting culture and social justice in career practices. In N. Arthur, R. Neault, & M. McMahon (Eds.), *Career theories and models at work: Ideas for practice* (pp. 21–30). CERIC.

Arthur, N., Collins, S., McMahon, M., & Marshall, C. (2009). Career practitioners' views of social justice and barriers for practice. *Canadian Journal of Career Development, 8*, 22–31. https://cjcd-rcdc.ceric.ca/index.php/cjcd/issue/view/21/22

Arthur, N., & McMahon, M. (Eds.) (2019). *Contemporary theories of career development: International perspectives*. Routledge.

Arthur, N., Neault, R., & McMahon, M. (Eds.). (2019). *Career theories and models at work: Ideas for practice*. CERIC.

Arulmani, G. (2019). The cultural preparedness framework: Equilibrium and its alteration. In N. Arthur & M. McMahon (Eds.), *Contemporary theories of career development: International perspectives* (pp. 195–208). Routledge.

Arulmani, G., & Kumar, S. (2023). Livelihood thinking for career development: Rethinking work from alternative perspectives. In D. Blustein & L. Flores (Eds.), *Rethinking work: Essays on building a better workplace* (pp. 15–19). Routledge.

Asrowi, A., Hanif, M., & Setiawan, B. (2021). Career development: The role of career counsellor towards job counselling. *International Journal of Instruction, 14*(1), 661–672. https:/doi.org/10.29333/iji.2021.14140a

Association of Service Providers for Employability and Career Training. (2022). *Advocacy*. https://aspect.bc.ca/Advocacy

Bakshi, A. J., & Fialho, N. (2019). Life course theory: Ideas for career counsellors. In N. Arthur, R. Neault, & M. McMahon (Eds.), *Career theories and models at work: Ideas for practice* (pp. 31–40). CERIC.

Bassot, B. (2014). Enabling culturally sensitive career counseling through critically reflective practice: The role of reflective diaries in personal and professional development. In G. Arulmani, A. Bakshi, F. Leong, & A. Watts (Eds.), *Handbook of career development. International and cross-cultural psychology* (pp. 453–464). Springer. https://doi.org/10.1007/978-1-4614-9460-7_25

Bassot, B. (2016). *The reflective practice guide: An interdisciplinary approach to critical reflection.* Routledge. https://doi.org/10.4324/9781315768298

Bernes, K. (2019). Implementing the synergistic theory of organizational career development. In N. Arthur, R. Neault, & M. McMahon (Eds.), *Career theories and models at work: Ideas for practice* (pp. 41–51). CERIC.

Bezanson, L., O'Reilly, E., & Magnusson, K. (2009). *Pan-Canadian mapping study of the career development sector*. Report submitted to the Forum of Labour Market Ministers Career Development Services Working Group. https://ccdf. ca/wp-content/uploads/2019/02/PAN-CANADIAN-MAPPING-STUDY-OF-THE-CAREER-DEVELOPMENT-SECTOR.pdf

Bimrose, J. (2019a). Choice or constraint? Sociological theory. In N. Arthur & M. McMahon (Eds.), *Contemporary theories of career development: International perspectives* (pp. 166–179). Routledge.

Bimrose, J. (2019b). Sociological career theory: Reframing choice. In N. Arthur, R. Neault, & M. McMahon (Eds.), *Career theories and models at work: Ideas for practice* (pp. 53–62). CERIC.

Bimrose, J., & Goddard, T. (2021). *The career development profession in Canada and the emergence of online/multi-modal practice delivery*. Blueprint & Future Skills Centre. https://fsc-ccf.ca/wp-content/uploads/2021/11/FSC-RCP-Profession-EN.pdf

Blustein, D. L., & Duffy, R. D. (2021) Psychology of working theory. In S. D. Brown & R. W. Lent (Eds.), *Career development and counseling: Putting theory and research to work* (3rd ed., pp. 201–235). Wiley.

Blustein, D., Duffy, R., Erby, W., & Kim, H. (2019). The psychology of working theory: A transformative approach to work and career. In N. Arthur, R. Neault, & M. McMahon (Eds.), *Career theories and models at work: Ideas for practice* (pp. 63–72). CERIC.

Blustein, D. L., Kenny, M. E., Di Fabio, A., & Guichard, J. (2019). Expanding the impact of the psychology of working: Engaging psychology in the struggle for decent work and human rights. *Journal of Career Assessment, 27*(1), 3–28. https://doi.org/10.1177/1069072718774002

Bordin, E. S. (1979). The generalizability of the psychoanalytic concept of the working alliance. *Psychotherapy: Theory, Research & Practice, 16,* 252–260.

Borgen, R. A. (Ed.). (2021). *Career development for diverse clients: Beyond the basics.* Cognella.

Britt, E., Sawatzky, R., & Swibaker, K. (2018). Motivational interviewing to promote employment. *Journal of Employment Counseling, 55*(4), 176–189. https://doi.org/10.1002/joec.12097

Britt, E., Soleymani, S., Wallace-Bell, M., & Garland, A. (2023). Motivational interviewing for employment: An exploration of practitioner skill and client change talk. *Journal of Employment Counseling, 60*(1), 42–59. https://doi.org/10.1002/joec.12198

Bronfenbrenner, U. (2000). Ecological systems theory. In A. E. Kazdin (Ed.), *Encyclopedia of psychology* (Vol. 3, pp. 129–133). Oxford University Press. https://doi.org/10.1037/10518-046

Brott, P. E. (2019). Narrative career counselling: The storied approach. In N. Arthur, R. Neault, & M. McMahon (Eds.), *Career theories and models at work: Ideas for practice* (pp. 73–82). CERIC.

Canadian Career Development Foundation. (n.d.). *Project background.* https://ccdp-pcdc.ca/en/project-background

Canadian Career Development Foundation. (2021a). *Pan-Canadian competency framework for career development professionals.* https://ccdp-pcdc.ca/media/competency_framework_downloads/competency_framework_downloads3.pdf

Canadian Career Development Foundation. (2021b). *Evidence for community employment services: A collaborative regional approach. Final report: A tale of transformation.* https://ccdf.ca/wp-content/uploads/2021/03/NLWIC-FINAL-REPORT-2021-04-01-CCDF-submitted.pdf

Canadian Career Development Foundation (2021c). *Code of ethics for career development professionals.* https://ccdp-pcdc.ca/en/pdf/Code_of_Ethics_2021_EN.pdf

Career Industry Council of Australia. (2019). *Professional standards for Australian career development practitioners.* https://cica.org.au/professional-standards/

Chan, C. K., & Hedden, L. N. (2023). The role of discernment and modulation in enacting occupational values: How career advising professionals navigate tensions with clients. *Academy of Management Journal, 66*(1), 276–305. https://doi.org/10.5465/amj.2020.1014

Chen, C. P., & Hong, J. W. L. (2019). Career self-determination theory in practice. In N. Arthur, R. Neault, & M. McMahon (Eds.), *Career theories and models at work: Ideas for practice* (pp. 83-92). CERIC.

Collins, S., Arthur, N., & Wong-Wiley, G. (2010). Enhancing reflective practice in multicultural counseling through cultural auditing. *Journal of Counseling & Development, 88*(3), 340–347. https://doi.org/10.1002/j.1556-6678.2010.tb00031.x

Commonwealth of Australia. (2022). *Australian blueprint for career development.* Commonwealth of Australia. https://content.yourcareer.gov.au/sites/default/files/2023-06/Australian-Blueprint-for-Career-Development.pdf

Conyers, L., Tackett, S., & Wright, S. (2022). Internal Medicine–Paediatrics residents' application of life design principles to career decisions. *Postgraduate Medical Journal, 98*(1164), 788–792. https://doi.org/10.1136/postgradmedj-2021-140094

Corey, G. (2019). *The art of integrative counselling.* American Counselling Association.

Cournoyer, L., & Lachance, L. (2019). Decision-action model: Overview and application to career development. In N. Arthur, R. Neault, & M. McMahon (Eds.), *Career theories and models at work: Ideas for practice* (pp. 93–101). CERIC.

de Bruin, G. P., & de Bruin, K. (2017). Career assessment. In G. B. Stead & M. B. Watson (Eds.), *Career psychology in the South African context* (3rd ed., pp. 185–193). Van Schaik.

Dionne, P., & Dupuis, A. (2019). Cultural-historical activity theory: Group career counselling for social justice of racialized women. In N. Arthur, R. Neault, & M. McMahon (Eds.), *Career theories and models at work: Ideas for practice* (pp. 103–113). CERIC.

do Céu Taveira, M., Cardoso, P., Silva, F., & Ribeiro, E. (2017). The therapeutic collaboration in life design counselling: The case of Ryan. *South African Journal of Education, 37*(4), Article 1466. https://doi.org/10.15700/saje.v37n4a1466

Domene, J. F., & Young, R. A. (2019). Career counselling using contextual action theory: Key concepts for practice. In N. Arthur, R. Neault, & M. McMahon (Eds.), *Career theories and models at work: Ideas for practice* (pp. 115–124). CERIC.

Dressler, R., Becker, S., Kawalilak, C., & Arthur, N. (2018). The cross-cultural reflection model for post-sojourn debriefing. *Reflective Practice, 19*(4), 490–504. https://doi:10.1080/14623943.2018.1530207

Egan, G. (2019). *The skilled helper: A problem-management and opportunity-development approach to helping*. Cengage Learning.

Evans, K. M., & Sejuit, A. L. (2021). *Gaining cultural competence in career counselling* (2nd ed.). National Career Development Association.

Féja, D., Csernátony, F., & Pais, A. (2023). Design thinking in career planning. Implementing tools and mindsets. *Il Capitale Culturale: Studies on the Value of Cultural Heritage,* Suppl.14/2023, 83–98. https://riviste.unimc.it/index.php/cap-cult/article/download/3137/2246

Flores, L. Y. (2009). Empowering life choices: Career counseling in the contexts of race and class. In N. Gysbers, M. J. Heppner, & J. A. Johnson (Eds.), *Career counselling: Contexts, processes, and techniques* (3rd ed., pp. 49–74). American Counselling Association.

Fuertes, J. N. (Ed.). (2022). *The other side of psychotherapy: Understanding clients' experiences and contributions in treatment.* American Psychological Association. https://doi.org/10.1037/0000303-000

Gergen, M. M., & Gergen, K. J. (2006). Narratives in action. *Narrative Inquiry,16*(1), 112–121. https://doi.org/10.1075/ni.16.1.15ger

Goodman, J. (2019). Schlossberg's 4S model of life transitions: Assessment and intervention planning. In N. Arthur, R. Neault, & M. McMahon (Eds.), *Career theories and models at work: Ideas for practice* (pp. 125–134). CERIC.

Gottfredson, L. S. (2005). Applying Gottfredson's theory of circumscription and compromise in career guidance and counseling. In S. D. Brown & R. W. Lent (Eds.), *Career development and counseling: Putting theory and research to work* (pp. 71-100). John Wiley.

Government of Canada. (n.d.a) *Plain language, accessibility, and inclusive communications.* https://www.canada.ca/en/privy-council/services/communications-community-office/communications-101-boot-camp-canadian-public-servants/plain-language-accessibility-inclusive-communications.html

Government of Canada. (n.d.b). *Skills for success.* https://www.canada.ca/en/services/jobs/training/initiatives/skills-success.html

Goyer, L., & Dumas, M.-P. (2019). My career GPS: A self-orienting career model for people and organizations. In N. Arthur, R. Neault, & M. McMahon (Eds.), *Career theories and models at work: Ideas for practice* (pp. 135–145). CERIC.

Hammond, M. S. (2014, April 1). *Helping clients change: The stages of change model and career development work.* National Career Development Association. https://www.ncda.org/aws/NCDA/pt/sd/news_article/87526/_PARENT/CC_layout_details/false

Healy, M., & McIlveen, P. (2019). My career chapter: The dialogical self as author and editor of a career autobiography. In N. Arthur, R. Neault, & M. McMahon (Eds.), *Career theories and models at work: Ideas for practice* (pp. 147–157). CERIC.

Herr, E. L. (2000). Collaboration, partnership, policy, and practice in career development. *The Career Development Quarterly, 48*(4), 293–300. https://doi.org/10.1002/j.2161-0045.2000.tb00874.x

Holland, J. L. (1985). *The self-directed search: A guide to educational and vocational planning.* Psychological Assessment Resources.

Holland, J. L. (1997). *Making vocational choices: A theory of vocational personalities and work environments* (3rd ed.). Psychological Assessment Resources.

Hooley, T., Sultana, R., & Thomsen, R. (Eds.). (2019). *Career guidance for emancipation: Reclaiming justice for the multitude.* Routledge.

Howard, K. A. S., & Dinius, S. M. (2019). Children's reasoning about career development: The conceptions of career choice and attainment model. In N. Arthur, R. Neault, & M. McMahon (Eds.), *Career theories and models at work: Ideas for practice* (pp. 159–169). CERIC.

Inge, K. J., Sima, A. P., Riesen, T., Wehman, P., & Brooks-Lane, N. (2023). The essential elements of customized employment: Results from a national survey of employment providers. *Rehabilitation Counseling Bulletin, 66*(3), 170–185. https://doi.org/10.1177/00343552221088256

International Association for Educational and Vocational Guidance. (2017). *IAEVG ethical guidelines.* https://iaevg.com/Ethical-guidelines

International Association for Educational and Vocational Guidance. (2018). *International competencies for educational and vocational guidance practitioners.* https://iaevg.com/competencies

International Labour Organization. (2019). *Time to act for SDG 8: Integrating decent work, sustained growth and environmental integrity.* https://www.ilo.org/global/publications/books/WCMS_712685/lang--en/index.htm

International Plain Language Federation. (n.d.). https://www.iplfederation.org/

Kattelus, M. (2019). KIPINÄ: SPARKS career counselling. In N. Arthur, R. Neault, & M. McMahon (Eds.), *Career theories and models at work: Ideas for Practice* (pp. 171–182). CERIC.

Khalijian, S., Pordelan, N., Khamsehzadeh, S., Askari, A., & Heydari, H. (2023). Customization and use of digital storytelling in providing online career counseling services to students with physical-motor disabilities: A mixed study. *Education and Information Technologies.* https://doi.org/10.1007/s10639-023-11658-z

Kijima, R., Yang-Yoshihara, M., & Maekawa, M. S. (2021). Using design thinking to cultivate the next generation of female STEAM thinkers. *International Journal of STEM Education, 8*(1), Article 14. https://doi.org/10.1186/s40594-021-00271-6

Kolb, D. A. (1984). *Experiential learning: Experience as the source of learning and development*. Prentice Hall.

Lengelle, R., Meijers, F., & Bonnar, C. (2019). Poetic creativity: The career writing method for professional reflectivity in the 21st century. In N. Arthur, R. Neault, & M. McMahon (Eds.), *Career theories and models at work: Ideas for practice* (pp. 183–193). CERIC.

Lent, R. W. (2017). Integration of theory, research and practice: A social cognitive perspective. In J. P. Sampson Jr., E. Bullock-Yowell, V. C. Dozier, D. S. Osborn, & J. G. Lenz (Eds.), *Integrating theory, research and practice in vocational psychology: Current status and future directions* (pp. 20–27). Florida State University. https://doi.org/10.17125/svp2016.ch1

Lent, R. W., & Brown, S. D. (2021). Career development and counseling: An introduction. In S. D. Brown & R. W. Lent (Eds.), *Career development and counseling: Putting theory and research to work* (3rd ed., pp. 1–29). Wiley.

Lin, Q., & Wang, C. (2022). Construction of the educational model of vocational college students' career planning based on design thinking. *Ergonomics in Design, 47*. AHFE Open Access. https://doi.org/10.54941/ahfe1001912

Luken, T., & de Folter, A. (2019). Acceptance and commitment therapy fuels innovation of career counselling. In N. Arthur, R. Neault, & M. McMahon (Eds.), *Career theories and models at work: Ideas for practice* (pp. 195–205). CERIC.

Magnusson, K., & Redekopp, D. E. (2019). Coherent career practice: A framework to organise career development concepts and practices. In N. Arthur, R. Neault, & M. McMahon (Eds.), *Career theories and models at work: Ideas for practice* (pp. 207–216). CERIC.

Maree, J. G. (2019). Career construction theory and its application. In N. Arthur, R. Neault, & M. McMahon (Eds.), *Career theories and models at work: Ideas for practice* (pp. 217–226). CERIC.

McCoy, L. (2019). Conceptualizing athletic career transitions with the holistic athletic career model. In N. Arthur, R. Neault, & M. McMahon (Eds.), *Career theories and models at work: Ideas for practice* (pp. 227–236). CERIC.

McIlveen, P., & Patton, W. (2010). My career chapter as a tool for reflective practice. *International Journal for Educational and Vocational Guidance, 10*(3), 147–160. https://doi.org/10.1007/s10775-010-9181-0

McKenzie, S., & Goddard, T. (2021). *Incenting responsive career pathways*. Blueprint & Future Skills Centre. https://fsc-ccf.ca/wp-content/uploads/2021/11/FSC-RCP-Roadmap-EN.pdf

McMahon, M. (2019a). *Does theory matter to the practice of career development?* https://careerwise.ceric.ca/2019/02/08/does-theory-matter-to-the-practice-of-career-development/#.ZGNu46VByUk

McMahon, M. (2019b). Qualitative career assessment: A higher profile in the 21st century? In J. A. Athanasou & H. N. Perera (Eds.), *International handbook of career guidance* (2nd ed., pp. 735–794). Springer.

McMahon, M., & Arthur, N. (2018). Career development theory: Origins and history. In N. Arthur & M. McMahon (Eds.), *Contemporary theories of career development: International perspectives* (pp. 3–19). Routledge.

McMahon, M., Bimrose, J., Watson, M., & Abkhezr, P. (2020). Integrating storytelling and quantitative career assessment. *International Journal for Educational and Vocational Guidance, 20*, 523–542. https://doi.org/10.1007/s10775-019-09415-1

McMahon, M., & Patton, W. (2019). The systems theory framework of career development: Applying systems thinking to career development theory and practice. In N. Arthur, R. Neault, & M. McMahon (Eds.), *Career theories and models at work: Ideas for practice* (pp. 237–247). CERIC.

McMahon, M., & Patton, W. (2000). Career counsellors, support, and lifelong learning: A case for clinical supervision. *International Journal for the Advancement of Counselling, 22,* 157–169. https://doi.org/10.1023/A:1005632604793

McWhirter, E. H., & McWha-Hermann. (2021). Social justice and career development: Progress, problems, and possibilities, *Journal of Vocational Behavior, 126*, Article 103492. https://doi.org/10.1016/j.jvb.2020.103492

Micheli, P., Wilner, S. J. S., Bhatti, S. H., Mura, M., & Beverland, M. B. (2019). Doing design thinking: Conceptual review, synthesis, and research agenda. *Journal of Product Innovation Management, 36*(2), 124–148. https://doi.org/10.1111/jpim.12466

Miller, J. H. (2019). Solution-focused theory and career practice. In N. Arthur, R. Neault, & M. McMahon (Eds.), *Career theories and models at work: Ideas for practice* (pp. 249–259). CERIC.

Millner, U. C., Brandt, D., Chan, L., Jette, A., Marfeo, E., Ni, P., Rasch, E., & Rogers, E. S. (2020). Exploring counselor-client agreement on clients' work capacity in established and consultative dyads. *Journal of Employment Counseling, 57*(3), 98–114. https://doi.org/10.1002/joec.12148

Milot-Lapointe, F., Savard, R., & Le Corff, Y. (2020). Effect of individual career counseling on psychological distress: Impact of career intervention components, working alliance, and career indecision. *International Journal for Educational and Vocational Guidance, 20*(2), 243–262. https://doi.org/10.1007/s10775-019-09402-6

Nauta, M. M. (2019). Holland's theory of career choice: Matching personalities and environments. In N. Arthur, R. Neault, & M. McMahon (Eds.), *Career theories and models at work: Ideas for practice* (pp. 261–270). CERIC.

Neary, S., & Johnson, C. (2016). *CPD for the career development professional: A handbook for enhancing practice*. Trotman.

Neault, R. A., & Pickerell, D. A. (2019) Career engagement: A conceptual model for aligning challenge and capacity. In N. Arthur, R. Neault, & M. McMahon (Eds.), *Career theories and models at work: Ideas for practice* (pp. 271–281). CERIC.

Niles, S. G., Amundson, N., & Yoon, H. J. (2019). Hope action theory: Creating and sustaining hope in career development. In N. Arthur, R. Neault, & M. McMahon (Eds.), *Career theories and models at work: Ideas for practice* (pp. 283–293). CERIC.

Olry-Louis, I. (2018). Expression and management of emotions in career counselling interactions. *British Journal of Guidance & Counselling, 46*(5), 616–631. https://doi.org/10.1080/03069885.2018.1483006

Osborn, D. S., Dozier, V. C., Bullock Yowell, E., Hayden, S. C. W., & Sampson, J. P., Jr. (2019). Cognitive information processing theory: Applying theory and research to practice. In N. Arthur, R. Neault, & M. McMahon (Eds.), *Career theories and models at work: Ideas for practice* (pp. 295–306). CERIC.

Osborn, D., Dozier, C., Peterson, G. W., Bullock-Yowell, E., Saunders, D. E., & Sampson, J. P., Jr. (2019). Cognitive information processing theory: Applications of an empirically based theory and interventions to diverse populations. In N. Arthur & M. McMahon (Eds.), *Contemporary theories of career development: International perspectives* (pp. 61–77). Routledge.

Palmer, R., & Klinga, S. (2022). A program exemplar – In Motion and Momentum: Building resilience, hope, and sustainable futures. In R. A. Borgen (Ed.), *Career development for diverse clients: Beyond the basics* (pp. 217–226). Cognella.

Parsons, F. (1909). *Choosing a vocation*. Houghton Mifflin.

Pasolli, K., & Cummings, S. (2021). *The role of employers in responsive career pathways*. Blueprint & Future Skills Centre. https://fsc-ccf.ca/wp-content/uploads/2021/11/FSC-RCP-RoleofEmpl-EN.pdf

Patton, W., & McMahon, M. (2021). *Career development and systems theory: Connecting theory and practice* (4th ed.). Brill.

Peavy, R. V. (2004). *SocioDynamic counselling: A practical approach to meaning making*. Taos Institute.

Phillips Davis, R. (2023). Working to survive, thrive, or something more? In D. Blustein & L. Flores (Eds.), *Rethinking work: Essays on building a better workplace* (pp. 20–24). Routledge.

Picard, F., Turcotte, M., Viviers, S., & Dionne, P. (2019). Career development practices from the capabilities perspective of social justice. In N. Arthur, R. Neault, & M. McMahon (Eds.), *Career theories and models at work: Ideas for Practice* (pp. 307–316). CERIC.

Pickerell, D. A., & Neault, R. A. (2012). *Where's the work? Helping career practitioners explore their career options*. Life Strategies. https://lifestrategies.ca/docs/Where's_the_Work_2012.pdf

Poehnell, G. (2019). Hope-filled engagement: New possibilities in life/career counselling. In N. Arthur, R. Neault, & M. McMahon (Eds.), *Career theories and models at work: Ideas for practice* (pp. 317–326). CERIC.

Popadiuk, N. (2019). Relational-cultural theory: Exploring how relationships influence career development. In N. Arthur, R. Neault, & M. McMahon (Eds.), *Career theories and models at work: Ideas for practice* (pp. 327–336). CERIC.

Pope, M. (2019). The career counselling with underserved populations model in practice. In N. Arthur, R. Neault, & M. McMahon (Eds.), *Career theories and models at work: Ideas for practice* (pp. 337–346). CERIC.

Prochaska, J.O. & DiClemente, C.C. (1982). Transtheoretical therapy: Toward a more integrative model of change. *Psychotherapy: Theory, Research & Practice, 19* (3), 276–288. https://doi.org/10.1037/h0088437

Pryor, R., & Bright, J. (2019a). Careers as fractal patterns: The chaos theory of careers perspective. In N. Arthur & M. McMahon (Eds.), *Contemporary theories of career development: International perspectives* (pp. 135–152). Routledge.

Pryor, R. G. L., & Bright, J. E. H. (2019b). Chaos theory for career counsellors. In N. Arthur, R. Neault, & M. McMahon (Eds.), *Career theories and models at work: Ideas for Practice* (pp. 347–357). CERIC.

Richardson, M. S. (2019). Counselling/psychotherapy: Bringing a vocational perspective into psychotherapy practice. In N. Arthur, R. Neault, & M. McMahon (Eds.), *Career theories and models at work: Ideas for practice* (pp. 359–368). CERIC.

Riverin-Simard, D., & Simard, Y. (2019). The continuous participation model: The ever-evolving perception of work. In N. Arthur, R. Neault, & M. McMahon (Eds.), *Career theories and models at work: Ideas for practice* (pp. 369–377). CERIC.

Robertson, F. (2009). The Johari window. In M. Wright (Ed.), *Gower handbook of internal communication* (2nd ed., pp. 163–168). Routledge.

Rogers, C. R. (1951). *Client-centered therapy*. Houghton-Mifflin.

Savickas, M. L. (Ed.) (2013). *Ten ideas that changed career development.* National Career Development Association. https://www.ncda.org/aws/NCDA/asset_manager/get_file/71112?ver=40196

Savickas, M. L. (2021). Career construction theory and counseling model. In S. D. Brown & R. W. Lent (Eds.), *Career development and counseling: Putting theory and research to work* (3rd ed., pp. 165–199). Wiley.

Schön, D. A. (1992). *The reflective practitioner: How professionals think in action.* Basic Books.

Sheu, H-B., & Wang, X. T. (2019). Social cognitive career theory: Overview and practical applications. In N. Arthur, R. Neault, & M. McMahon (Eds.), *Career theories and models at work: Ideas for practice* (pp. 379–389). CERIC.

Spangar, T. (2019). SocioDynamic career counselling. In N. Arthur, R. Neault, & M. McMahon (Eds.), *Career theories and models at work: Ideas for practice* (pp. 391–400). CERIC.

Spinelli, L. (2022). Customizing your career path. Talent Development, 76(8), 56–61. https://go.exlibris.link/slGGNDmP

Straub, C., Vinkenburg, C. J., & van Kleef, M. (2020). Career customization: Putting an organizational practice to facilitate sustainable careers to the test. *Journal of Vocational Behavior, 117*, Article 103320. https://doi.org/10.1016/j.jvb.2019.103320

Sultana, R. G. (2022). Four 'dirty words' in career guidance: From common sense to good sense. *International Journal of Educational and Vocational Guidance.* https://doi.org/10.1007/s10775-022-09550-2

Super, D. E. (1990). A life-span, life-space approach to career development. In D. Brown & L. Brooks (Eds.), *Career choice and development: Applying contemporary theories to practice* (2nd ed., pp. 197–261). Jossey-Bass.

Swanson, J. L., & Fouad, N. A. (2015*). Career theory and practice: Learning through case studies* (3rd ed.). Sage.

Tang, M. (2019). Ecological career counselling model: Enhancing accordance of person and environment for a meaningful life. In N. Arthur, R. Neault, & M. McMahon (Eds.), *Career theories and models at work: Ideas for practice* (pp. 401–410). CERIC.

Thomson, E. F., King-Nyberg, B., Morris-Reade, J., Taylor, C., & Borgen, R. (2021). A needs assessment of virtual career practitioners. *Canadian Journal of Career Development, 21*(1), 79–92. https://cjcd-rcdc.ceric.ca/index.php/cjcd/issue/view/35/38

Toh, R., & Sampson, J. P. (2021). Improving public employment service delivery in developing countries: Right servicing through the cognitive information processing approach. *British Journal of Guidance & Counselling, 49*(1), 90–103. https://doi.org/10.1080/03069885.2019.1577357

United Nations. (2015). *Transforming our world: The 2030 agenda for sustainable development.* https://sdgs.un.org/publications/transforming-our-world-2030-agenda-sustainable-development-17981 van Brussel, G. (2019). The space model for intrapreneurship: Facilitating development of a new career role. In N. Arthur, R. Neault, & M. McMahon (Eds.), *Career theories and models at work: Ideas for practice* (pp. 411–422). CERIC.

Verganti, R., Dell'Era, C., & Swan, K. S. (2021). Design thinking: Critical analysis and future evolution. *Journal of Product Innovation Management, 38*(6), 603–622. https://doi.org/10.1111/jpim.12610

Viviers, S. (2019). Taking care of oneself by taking care of one's work: A clinical and critical perspective on work and mental health. In N. Arthur, R. Neault, & M. McMahon (Eds.), *Career theories and models at work: Ideas for practice* (pp. 423–431). CERIC.

Vondracek, F. W., & Ford, D. H. (2019). The living systems theory of vocational behaviour and development. In N. Arthur, R. Neault, & M. McMahon (Eds.), *Career theories and models at work: Ideas for practice* (pp. 433–441). CERIC.

Vygotsky, L. S. (1978). *Mind in society: The development of higher psychological processes*. Harvard University Press.

Watson, M. (2017). Career constructivism and culture: Deconstructing and constructing career counselling. In M. McMahon (Ed.), *Career counselling: Constructivist approaches* (2nd ed., pp. 43-53). Routledge.

Watson, M. (2019a). The career development assessment and counselling model of Donald Super. In N. Arthur, R. Neault, & M. McMahon (Eds.), *Career theories and models at work: Ideas for practice* (pp. 443–452). CERIC.

Watson, M. (2019b). The reciprocal relationship of career theory and practice. In N. Arthur & M. McMahon (Eds.), *Contemporary theories of career development: International perspectives* (pp. 20–30). Routledge.

Watson, M., & McMahon, M. (2015). An introduction to career assessment. In McMahon, M., & Watson, M. (Eds.), *Career assessment: Qualitative approaches* (pp. 3–11). Sense.

Watson, M., & McMahon, M. (2017). Adult career counselling: Narratives of adaptability and resilience. In K. Maree (Ed.), *Psychology of career adaptability, employability and resilience* (pp. 189–204). Springer. https://doi.org/10.1007/978-3-319-66954-0_12

Whiston, S. C., Rossier, J., & Hernandez Barón, P. M. (2016). The working alliance in career counseling: A systematic overview. *Journal of Career Assessment, 24*(4), 591–604. https://doi.org/10.1177/1069072715615849

Williams, B. (2003). The worldview dimensions of individualism and collectivism: Implications for counselling. *Journal of Counseling & Development, 81*(3), 370–374. https://doi.org/10.1002/j.1556-6678.2003.tb00263.x

Williams, R. G., Baker, S. B., & Williams-DeVane, C. R. (2018). Effects of customized counseling interventions on career and college readiness self-efficacy of three female foster care youth. *The Professional Counselor, 8*(2), 159–174. https://doi.org/10.15241/rgw.8.2.159

Wolfe, D. M., & Kolb, D. A. (1980). Career development, personal growth, and experiential learning. In J. W. Springer (Ed.), *Issues in career and human resource development* (pp. 1–11). American Society for Training and Development.

Woodend, J. (2019). The theory of work adjustment: Seeking and maintaining satisfaction and satisfactoriness. In N. Arthur, R. Neault, & M. McMahon (Eds.), *Career theories and models at work: Ideas for practice* (pp. 453–462). CERIC.

Yates, J., & Hooley, T. (2018). Advising on career image: Perspectives, practice and politics. *British Journal of Guidance & Counselling, 46*(1), 27–38. https://doi.org/10.1080/03069885.2017.1286635